Zacharias Collin

An Essay on the Scoto-English Dialect

Part I.: Along with Some French and German Theses...

Zacharias Collin

An Essay on the Scoto-English Dialect
Part I.: Along with Some French and German Theses...

ISBN/EAN: 9783337086510

Printed in Europe, USA, Canada, Australia, Japan

Cover: Foto ©Thomas Meinert / pixelio.de

More available books at **www.hansebooks.com**

An Essay
on
The Scoto-English Dialect.

Part I.
An Academical Dissertation.

Along with some French and German Theses,

With the Permission of the Philosoph. Faculty of Lund,

to be publicly defended

by

ZACHARIAS COLLIN M. A.

in the Lecture-Hall N:o 1, on the 5th of March, 1862,
at 10 o'clock, A. M.

Lund.
Berlings Printing Office.
1862.

I.

M. Chevallet .(Origine et Formation de la Langue Française, I. p. 216), après avoir relevé les fautes dans lesquelles sont tombés les auteurs qui ont essayé à tirer un grand nombre de mots Français des langues Celtiques, — dit qu'il ne donne comme des mots Celtiques que ceux "qui ne se trouvant ni dans le Latin, ni dans trois idiomes Germaniques, ont été conservés au moins dans deux idiomes Neo-Celtiques". — Ce raisonnement n'est pas juste, parce qu'on trouve dans les idiomes Germaniques un nombre assez considérable de mots qui, selon toute probabilité, doivent être référés aux langues Celtiques, et, par conséquent, on donne pour des mots Germaniques un plus ou moins grand nombre qui ne le sont point du tout.

II.

Les règles que donnent, de nos jours, les grammairiens Français pour l'usage du participe présent ne s'accordent pas avec la pratique des siècles passés.

III.

Il serait d'une très grande utilité pour les jeunes gens qui s'appliquent à la philologie d'avoir des dictionnaires dressés d'une telle manière que les dérivés se trouvent toujours sous leurs racines respectives. Cet arrangement permettrait d'embrasser d'un coup d'oeil tous les mots rattachés les uns aux autres par un lien de parenté.

I.

Vor etwa achtzig Jahren gab ein Schotte, Namens Pinkerton, ein dickes Buch heraus, in welchem er zu beweisen suchte, dass die Schotten einer anderen Herstammung als die südlichen

Engländer wären. Seine Theorie lief darauf hinaus, die Pikten (er streicht das *T* dieses Namens und leitet ihn dann von Wiken, dem alten Namen Bohus-läns, ab), und somit auch die gegenwärtigen Bewohner der schottischen Niederlande als Nachkommen jener Pikten zu Skandinaviern zu machen. So unverdaulich diese Theorie, mit Betrachtungen anderer Art zusammengehalten, auch scheinen mag, hat sie dennoch Anhänger gefunden, und, so wenig auch das, was nur aus der Luft gegriffen ist, einer Widerlegung bedarf, hat es doch Personen gegeben, die sich mit der Widerlegung dieses Hirngespinstes abgaben. Hierbei hat man sich vorzugsweise der skandinavischen Sprache bedient, und von der mittelalterlichen und jetzigen Nichtübereinstimmung derselben mit der Sprache der schottischen Niederlande, auf das Nichtherstammen dieser Sprache von der skandinavischen geschlossen. Dieser Schluss ist durch und durch unberechtigt.

II.

Die Behauptung, dass die celtischen Sprachen dem indoeuropäischen Sprachstamme nicht angehören, ist ganz unbegründet.

III.

Ganz wie in den Onomatopöen die Zeitdauer des Lautes, den sie nachahmen, durch Vocale, deren Aussprechen einer längeren oder kürzeren Zeit bedarf, angedeutet wird, scheint bei der Bildung der Verba, zumal der starken, auf dasselbe Verhältniss Rücksicht genommen zu sein. Ebenso scheint der Ablaut auch darauf berechnet die Zeitdauer einer Handlung oder eines Zustandes anzudeuten. So deutet das *i* des Infin. und Pres. auf das Augenblickliche; das *a* des Praeteriti auf das Fortwährende, und das *u* des Participii perfect. auf das Abgeschlossene der Handlung, hin.

Girdled round by the ocean, as they are, the British Isles have not always in its waves had their friends and protectors. The British poet could not in every age, in the exulting pride of unrivalled power, sing: "Britannia needs no bulwark, No tower on the steep."

On the contrary, her fates confirm the truthfulness of the old saying: the seas unite, and do not divide. Repeatedly invaded, and, when invaded, always conquered, she has seen one people after another overwhelm her inhabitants, the new-comers themselves to be in their order supplanted by new intruders. In this way, the stock of her population has become one of the most mixed in Europe. The under-current of its blood is Celtic, but into this current Romans, Saxons (o: Low-German tribes), Danes, Norwegians, and Norman-French, have, by successive transfusions, poured theirs in more or less mighty streams. Even the Britons themselves were, perhaps, encroachers upon an earlier population. More than one scholar has, at least, been inclined to see traces of the Gaëls in such parts of England where history knows nothing about them [1]). It is, however, difficult to affirm anything for certain, the annals of the Gaëls being stille darker than those af the Cymries, upon which the intercourse with the Romans, at least now and then, casts a straygleam of historical light. The Gaëls, as the heroes of Ossian, walk in the dark. As long as they, in wild and barbarous independence, kept quiet in the rugged mountainglens af Scotland and the bogs of Ire-

---

[1]) M'LAUCHLAN, Celtic Gleanings, p. 44; cf. GARNETT'S Philological Essays, pp. 151, 196.

land, the Romans took no interest in them [2]). First when the Roman empire, lingering in an artificially protracted agony, had lost the power to protect its subjects, we see them issue forth from their retreats to fall upon their southern neighbours, the Romanized Britons, whom a slavery of 400 years had made little able to wield the weapons, their lords, on the eve of leaving the island, had put into their hands with the advice to defend themselves. But the giving back of weapons the use of which the Romans, in the days of their power, had forbidden, was not sufficient. The skill to use them, the courage to stand unflinching in the battle, were gone. Continually defeated by their enemies, the Britons, in whose ranks also civil disorders seem to have immediately succeeded the taking away of the Roman pressure, found themselves unable to resist. Their cries of despair went to Rome. Repellunt barbari ad mare, repellit mare ad barbaros, inter hoc oriuntur duo genera funerum, aut jugulamur aut mergimur — were the words in which they addressed Aetius [3]). But the wretchedness of the eternal city was as great as theirs: she could not any more protect the nations her tyranny and mortified civilisation had effeminated. These must now shift for themselves, and look for help from anywhere else. — The Britons cast their eyes on the sons of Germany, and, invited by Vortigern, the Saxons came over to England, for which now a new stadium of historical development took its beginning.

[2]) To give an account of the opinions that are, or have been, current among historians and antiquaries on behalf of the ancient Celtic inhabitants of Britain would lead us too far, and is, besides, of a very inferior interest to our purpose. We therefore content ourselves with referring the reader to the following works:
  CHALMERS: Caledonia (vol. 1).
  PINKERTON: An Enquiry into the History of Scotland preceeding the reign of Malcolm III.
  JAMIESON: Introduction to his Scottish Dictionary.
  LATHAM: Ethnology of the British Isles.
  SKENE: The Highlanders of Scotland.
  ZEUSS: Die Deutschen und die Nachbarstämme.
  WILSON: Archaelogy and Prehistoric Annals of Scotland.
[3]) GILDAS (ed. Stevenson) De excidio Britanniae Cap. XIII.

Some authors are of opinion that German colonists had taken up their abodes in England already during the Roman dominion⁴). They have also, I think, produced sufficient evidence to prove that they are right; but yet it seems to me the ancient accounts are not invalidated, the state of matters in England as well as on the continent of Europe, at this time, powerfully pleading their cause, and making it extremely probable that the transmigrations from the coasts of Germany just about the midst of the 5:th century were made on a larger scale than ever before or after this time. We may question many of the fabulous traditions, but the exactness of the main facts cannot reasonably be doubted. We may shake our heads at the genealogies of Gildas, but have no right to declare the history of Hengist and Horsa to be mere allegorical myths. What improbality is there in the narration of the leaders of some Saxon bands that crossed the Northsea and settled in England bearing names still in use among the inhabitants of Friesland?⁵).

The Saxons had given their plighted faith to defend the Britons against their enemies; on consequent they must have been placed where their services were of most avail. This must have been in the very vicinity of these enemies, in order to prevent their inroads upon the British territory⁶). We may, thence, suppose that the northern boundaries, facing the Picts and Scots, were very early abandoned to the newcomers. This is not mere supposition. In the Historia Britonum which goes under the name of NENNIUS we find a passage, interesting in more than one point of view⁷). Hengist advised Vortigern to

---

⁴) SCHAUMANN in: Göttinger Studien, 1845. p. 337. cf. his Geschichte des niedersächsischen Volks, p. 25; KEMBLE, The Saxons in England, 1 vol. p. 7 f.; LATHAM, Handbook of the English Langu. part. 1.

⁵) HALBERTSMA, Introduct. to Dr. BOSWORTH'S A. S. Dictionary, p. LIV.

⁶) But why settled Saxons also in the southernmost parts of England? Was it because there existed, as Schanmann (l. c.) thinks, a British littus Saxonicum, occupied by Germans hostile to the Britons?

⁷) Historia Britonum (ed. Stevenson) cap. 38.

invite his son and the son of his brother, and settle them and their followers on the Scottish borders. The British chief listened to the counsel. Octha and Ebissa came to the call with forty ships filled with warlike comrades: sailed round the land of the Picts, laid waste the isles of Orkney, and settled themselves finally in those regions which now bear the name of the Scotch Lowlands [8]). It's true that Nennius is not regarded as a first-rate historical authority, but here he may perhaps be trusted, the consideration of what was the natural policy of the Britons confirming his veracity [9]).

Bye and bye — may it have been brought about through the perfidy with which the traditions charge Hengist, who, upon finding himself at ease in Britain, sent to his native country for reinforcements; or may it have been caused by the general movement among the European nations, which at this time seems to have pressed hard upon the populations of the German westcoasts — Britain was filled with Low-German bands that soon got into possession of the territory from the southcoast to the friths of Forth and of Clyde, the ancient inhabitants maintaining themselves only in those districts where mountain-strongholds gave a temporary shelter from the pursuits of their enemies. — Although it be impossible satisfactorily to account for the ethnographical relations of the latter, from the well known and uncontestable fact of the nations of antiquity and the middle ages being split into a multiplicity of divisions and subdivisions, differing more or less in point of language and customs, we may conclude, that such diversities also prevailed among the conquerors of Britain. The state of things which these etablished in their new country [1]) did rather tend to increase than to diminish those

[8]) We will in the sequel come back to this passage of Nennius, when we shall have to treat the Saxonizing of Scotland.

[9]) For an early German colonisation of the Scotch Lowlands speaks also the inscription of a tombstone, digged up, some years ago, at Kirkliston, a few miles to the south of Edinburgh, and preserved in the Museum of the Society of Scottish Antiquaries of that town. It runs thus: IN (H)OC TUMULO IACET VETTA F VICTA.

These names, I think, are only found among the first conquerors

[1]) The seven, I think, were not the greatest number of their kingdoms.

differences, and we have every reason to believe that there existed a good many provincial dialects [2]). These dialects, however, ranged themselves under three principal heads: the dialects of the South [3]), the Midlands, and the North [4]). Passing the two first, we turn to the last, it being the very object of our researches.

BEDE [5]), and after him the A. S. Chronicle, speaking of the German conquest of Britain, says, that the foreign invaders came from three different nations: the Angles, the Jutes, and the Old-Saxons. The Angles settled in East Anglia, Mercia and to the north of the river Humber, the Jutes taking possession of Kent and the isle of Wight [6]), and the Saxons holding the rest of the new-conquered territory.

The three races, if races they may be called, were kindred in blood as well as in language. It is therefore no easy task to make out the differences between them, to separate from out the swarms of wandering nations who crowded along the frontiers of Christianized Europe those tribes to whom the conquerors properly belonged. This is, however, to us a very subordinate question. More interesting it would be to ascertain how far the Scandinavian tribes partook of the first migration to England, it being likely enough that some Scandinavians might

[2]) Hence the diversities of spelling in the A. S. M. S. S. — The dialects seem at least here to afford a more plausible ground of diversity than Mr. HALBERTSMA'S suggestion of the redundancy of diphthongal sounds being so great in A. S., that the authors vainly strove to express them in writing. Halbertsma, Introduct. to BOSW. A. S. Dict. p. XXXV.

[3]) The common West Saxon; under king Alfred promoted to language of the court, and hereby gaining a complete superiority as literary language.

[4]) It is to be remembered that each of these three dialects only shows itself with all characteristic marks in M. S. S. from the interior of its districts; when it comes, as it were, directly from the headquarters. Where the districts meet, also the dialects flow together; whence a great difficulty to determine the localities of a good number of M. S. S.

[5]) BEDE, Historia Ecclesiast. (ed. STEVENSON) lib. I. cap. 15. The Saxon Cronicle (ed. J. INGRAM) sub A. D. 449.

[6]) Concerning the Jutish settlement, see Latham, Ethnology of the British Isles, p. 232.

have joined the Angles [7]). Any evidence in this respect, however, has never been produced, and will in, all probability, never be. We shall not dwell upon it. Instead of wasting away our ink on windy guesses at possibilities, we pass over to England to see how the Angles accommodated themselves in their new country.

The kingdom of Northumberland (or, sometimes at least, the Northumbrian kingdoms) extended northwards as far as to the Frith of Forth. Its western boundaries are not to be determined. They were, as may be presumed, subject to continual alterations, dependent on the good or ill luck in the war waged upon the neighbours. The Northumbrian kings seem temporarily to have swayed the Britons of Strathclyde [8]), but that they ever ruled Galloway and Cumberland is by no means certain [9]). Their power seems in the 8th century to have reached its height, and some time thereafter to have begun decaying. —

[7]) What kind of people were the Angles themselves? As BEDE (1. c.) tells us that the whole Angl. population left their homesteads, we may conclude, that the present inhabitants of Angeln are no descendants of the Angli of the A. S. tradition, even granted that their land is its Angulus; cf. ZEUSS Die Deutschen und die Nachbarstämme, pp. 152, 495, and LATHAM, Ethnolog. of the Brit. Isles, p. 200.

[8]) CHALMERS, Caledonia, I, pp. 250—59. Ile tries [pp. 235—49] to show that the people of Strath — Clyde were Romanized Britons, and, consequently, also Picts, all Picts according to him being Britons. It is, however, doubtful, if his premises bear out the consequences. The truth lies perhaps here, as so often, in the midst.

[9]) I have, in the foregoing, alluded to a passage of NENNIUS, which appears referable to a German colonisation in these parts. Besides Nennius there is no author, that mentions anything to this purpose, and his authority would weigh little with me, were it not for the very great interest which the passage alluded to excites. Could it be proved, that such an ancient German settlement existed in the western Lowlands of Scotland, it would be completely decisive in point of the history of the Northumbrian dialect. This will appear, when we come to treat of the Ruthwell cross. — It must however be owned that a glance on the map of the district, recognizing among its local names the largest portion to be apparently of a Celtic origin, is not quite favourable to such a supposition. On the contrary, the small number of German names (the termination — ing is of rare occurrence) speak for its having been relatively late Germanized.

The Scots, having migrated into Caledonia, gradually got a superiority over the Northern as well as the Southern Picts, and formed a mighty kingdom [1]). The struggle between them and the Northumbrians, carried on for a long time, seems, towards the close of the 9th century, to have ended in the possessions of the latter to the north of the river Tweed having been wrested from them, to become an integrating part of the newborn Scottish monarchy.

The remainder of the Northumbrian provinces did not long enjoy the benefits of peace. The land between the Humber and the Tweed, at this time more advanced in civilisation than any other portion of Teutonic Europe [2]), and sprinkled all over with seats of learning and magnificent places of worship, was, from the very beginning of the Northmen's roving westwards, more than the other parts of England, exposed to the storms which from Scandinavia swept over the west of Europe. It is pitiful to read in the Chronicles the pictures of its state during the last years of the 8th and the whole of the three following centuries. Monasteries burnt, monks slain, armies annihilated, towns sacked, and the followers of the Raven, that now:

— — — "soared on high,
Triumphant through Northumbrian sky,"

year after year, unpunished, pitching their camps in the heart of the land, removing from those parts which their levies had reduced to the most miserable poverty to others, thitherto spared: such are the pictures disclosed by every page. In the lapse of time, however, many settled, and busied themselves in rebuilding what they a little before had pulled down. The infusion of Northman blood in this way was, doubtless, tolerably strong, and the effects of it too conspicuous to be overlooked by the chroniclers [3]). But even, if these had been silent, we should

---

[1]) Wilson, l. c. Part. IV. ch. 1.

[2]) Kemble, Archaeologia, vol. XXVIII p. 338; Innes, Scotland in the Middle Ages, p. 64.

[3]) — est enim ante hoc tempus et fuit diu Dacorum genere multum permixta illa provincia (Yorkshire) et multum assentanea in loquela. — Chronic. Joannis Wallingford. apud Gale, I, p. 548. — The following passage, as probably chiefly applying to Northumbria,

not entirely have wanted information, there being found in these regions lots of local names unanimously assigned to a Scandinavian origin [4]), while the dialects spoken in them still seem to

seems also worth notice. Ein var þa tunga i Einglandi sem i Danmarku ok Noregi, enn þá skiptust tungur i Einglandi er Vilhialmr Bastardr vann Eingland. Sagan af Gunnlaugi Ormstungu (Hauniæ 1774, 4:o) p. 86. Cf. also XLIV Pröver af Oldnordisk Sprog og Literatur, udgivne af KONR. GISLASON, p. 449.

[4]) WORSAAE, An Account of the Danes and Norwegians in England, Scotland and Ireland, p. 71, and passim. — It may, however, be questioned, if Mr. Worsaae does not lay too great stress upon the topographical etymology, it being generally admitted that no department of philology more swarms with difficulties than this. To show the truth of this, I will give a most striking instance in the name of the greatest town on earth. Supposed that we were quite ignorant of the history of London, we might as well derive its name from the Icelandic hlunnr (cylindricus ligneus, navi subducendæ subjectus, EGILSON) and tun (area septa, idm) as from the Cymric lun (ship) and dun (town; originally inclosure?). - It is necessary to look for how the etymologies agree with the general analogy of the vernacular language, not without strong reasons considering as foreign what as well may be home-made. The analogies may sometimes be few, but that gives no right of overlooking them. Keeping this in view, we will venture some few remarks on the terminations of local names supposed to be of a northern derivation.

Of these no one advances such pretensions on the honour of being acknowledged a good Scandinavian as *by*. Its root *buan* (N. A. bua or bya) is, however, of very frequent occurrence in A. S., particularly in the M. S. S. of the north; and its forming from the verb is not devoid of analogy. By is found as a word in its own right in a M. S. of the Gospels, preserved at Cambridge (Bosw. A. S. Dictionary, sub v. bye), and also in the Durham-book:

— se ðe haefde in byrgenum hus I lytelo bye. Li. Mr. 5, 3. Here I rather think it corresponding to the Old-Norse *bu*, which, if imported to England, had probably retained its original vowel. — The age of the last monument is known, as shall soon be shown, that of the Cambr. M. S. we ignore.

Þorpe is first found in the Sax. Chron., but, as common to all German dialects, it cannot, without further proofs, be registered as a Scandin. import. Cf. GRIMM, Gesch. der Deut. Spr. II, p. 630.

Þwaite (cf. the Swed. *tret;* IHRE, Gloss. Suio-Goth. sub v.) is likely to derive from the A. S. verb, þweotan (to cut off). — *Haugh*,

give evidence of their once having been influenced by the Old-Norse tongue.

But, even granted the Danish colonisations took place to a large extent, we have no evidence whatever to suppose their having proceeded so far as to supersede the exterminated ancient population. The Northmen swayed the land, but the majority of the people were Saxons, quite as, now-a-days, the bulk of the Northenglish dialects are of Anglic, and not of Scandinavian origin. Upon the whole, viewing the general results as they now present themselves, we must agree with that author of the Saxon Chronicle (p. 121) who said: Naefde se here, Godes þances, Angelcyn ealles for-swiðe gebrocod.

What the Danes had not been able to do in respect to the Angles, was no more done by the Norman-French to the joint population of Angles and Danes. Their political liberties, it is true, were suppressed, after many a year of hard struggle; their numbers were thinned by dint of dreadful decimations; Norman barons were favoured with feudal grants of their odal possessions, while foreign prelates were invested with their clerical

by Worsaae considered as the Iceland. *haugr*, is, at least sometimes, of another origin. SINCLAIR, Observations on the Scottish dialect, p. 193, and JAMIESON, Scottish Dictionary, sub v., explain it: a small meadow, which it also seems to mean in this verse:
— — scho went *doun* to the *haw*. Sevin Seages p. 31.
I leave undecided, if in the following verse *heuch* is our old haugr:
Kepand his bird under a heuch Amangis the holtis hair.
Rob. and Mak.

The etymology of *toft* seems dark; perhaps it may be referred to the A. S. þufe, a germ, sprout, whence þuwian, to put forth shoots, the change of þ into t not being uncommon.

Dale (sw. dal) is by BOSWORTH (A. S. Diction. sub. v.) quoted from Beowulf.

Beck (a rivulet, a brook) and *force* (sw. fors, a waterfall), are perhaps more dubious as A. S.

With reference to the local names af Northumbria, it may not be devoid of interest to mention that Ireland, where no Teutons settled before the Northmen, presents us with an exceedingly small number of names of a northern extraction. Among 3842, only 20 are Scandinavian. CHALMERS, Caled. I. p. 30.

dignities. Both clerks and barons took great pains to break the spirit of the North. But it was not broken; it had a greater force of resistance than the South, and lived on through centuries to support a whole series of rebellions against the descendants of its Norman tyrants. [5]). — The history of Scotland during these remote ages is involved in an utter darkness, seldom pierced through by a ray of light. The old Scotch historians, no doubt, tell us a good deal; their narrations partake only too much of the fabulous to be fully relied upon. It seems, however, tolerably certain, that the Northmen (here the Norwegians), although they seized upon the Orkney — and Western isles, and even contrived to colonize the northern half of the Highlands, were never able to gain a fast footing in the Lowlands, where their inroads always were efficaciously opposed by the Scotch kings [6]).

But the course of events, which led to the saxonizing of this country, is, although the Norwegians be excluded from any partnership in it, by no means clear. Wrested from the Northumbrian kings, the land to the north of the Tweed remained a possession of the Scottish crown. But were the Anglic inhabitants driven out in order to make room for settlers of the Gaëlic race? That would, indeed, have been a shortsighted policy, and it is very incredible that the Scotch kings would have banished from their territory a people in every respect superior to their own countrymen. On supposing the Angles having been permitted to remain in their ancient abodes, we are not forced to take refuge to such trifling arguments as those which GEDDES [7]) and CHALMERS have brought forth to account for the Low-

[5]) Cf. THIERRY, Histoire de la conquête d'Angleterre par les Normands.

[6]) In the Saxon Chron. we find, under A. D. 875, the following passage (if i am not mistaken, the only one found there mentioning invasions of Northmen on the territory of the Scotch Lowlands): (a host of Northmen) þ loud geode and of thergode on Peohtas and on Stræcled Wealas. — But an allusion to a Scandinavian settlement in these quarters I have neither discovered in the Saxon nor in any other chronicle I have had the opportunity of perusing.

[7]) Transactions of the Antiquaries of Scotl. I vol. p. 402. The

landers' speaking a Teutonic and not a Gaëlic dialect; we have neither to seek for the cause of this fact in the multitudes of Anglic captives, said by Malcolm Ceanmor to have been brought from England to become slaves in Scotland, nor in the influence of some courtiers, whose speech probably partook more of French than Anglo-Saxon [8]). — Taken for granted, then, that Angles remained in the Lowlands in the 9th and the following centuries, the question rises, to what extent they possessed them. To this we may safely answer, that their occupancy was confined to the Lothians; Galloway and Strath-Clyde being still occupied by their ancient Celtic populations. When and how these were dispossessed, is of little interest to us. Probably it was in the same way in which we see the German people of Scotland in our days encroaching upon the lands of their neighbours in the Highlands. Many a clan-chief (according to the Celtic ideas the representative of the founder of the family) did not scruple to apply to the English law for a writ that made him sole owner of the (according to the same ideas) common family-property; whereupon he gave his "children" [9]) warning to remove, in order to provide more spacious sheep-walks, or an opportunity of "high farming," yielding more money unto the paternal cash [1]) In our time the exiled Gaël leaves his native glen to the "Saxon", and wanders to America or Australia, where his labour is free as wellas his own person; in the middle — ages he must remain, often to be transformed from a free man into a glebæ adscriptus [2]).

As now into the Highlands, the Teutonic emigration in

conjecture of Chalmers, if i am right, is found in the 1 vol. of Caledonia, but want of access to that book now prevents quoting the page.

[8]) WARTON, History of English Poëtry, ed. PRICE, I, p. 3, in the note.

[9]) Clann means in Gaëlic children. See Mc ALPINE'S Gaël. Dictionary.

[1]) From the instinctive feeling of the Gaël, that he once will be altogether driven out of his territory by the "Sassenach', his inveterate hatred to the latter, so admirably painted by Sir WALTER SCOTT in the Lady of the Lake and Waverley, and often alluded to by the old writers, leads its origin.

[2]) TYTLER, History of Scotland, II, p. 532.

the remote centuries we are speaking of, may have found its way into the Celtic portions of the Lowlands. The stream of "Southrons," at first slow, was, when William the Conqueror had won England, immensely swelled, as well from those Saxons, who preferred leaving the homes of their ancestors to submitting to the Norman yoke, as from the Normans themselves, many of whom, discontented with William, left England to seek their fortune in Scotland [3]). Normans and Saxons met there on common ground and on an equal footing, and both were highly favoured by the Scottish kings, who immediately in the new-comers saw an excellent weapon against their unruly Celtic subjects [4]).

Here we presently stop sketching some shadowy outlines of Northumbrian history, which we thought necessary for the understanding of what we have to say of the North-English dialect. This we now have to consider: 1) as it presents itself prior to the year 1000, and 2) in its shape during the three centuries that preceded the succession of James VI to the English throne.

The Old North-Anglic [5]) Dialect.

We have already adverted to the remarkable fact of the Teutonic civilisation in Britain having put forth its first flowers in Northumbria. The most celebrated names that have come down to us connected with A. S. learning and genius, BEDA and CAEDMON, belonged both to Angles. The latter, who "was placed in worldly life until the time, that he was of mature

[3]) Thus, for instance, the families of Baliol and Bruce were both of Norman extraction.
[4]) Concerning what we have alluded to in the text, see some interesting extracts from the old accounts of the battle of the Standard in INNES' able book, Scotland in the Middle Ages, p. 94.
[5]) I prefer the denomination Anglic to Northumbrian, as reminding of the origin of the population to the north of the Humber; while the latter only indicates the locality where the Anglic dialect was spoken, without adverting to anything more.

age", and that, too, in a very low station [6]), was totally destitute of education, and would probably never have known the holy writings but for the interpretations of his cloister-brethren. He composed his songs in the Anglic language, this BEDA expressly tells us [7]), and we have good reason to believe that by Anglic Beda here means the dialect north of the Humber. But in this form we have them no more. The West Saxon having become the literary dialect, Caedmon's poems were translated into it, and of the original only a short fragment, first printed by WANLEY [8]), still exists.

Besides this, two fragments more have been discovered. The one, called the deathbed-verses of Beda, is preserved in an ancient M. S. at St. Gallen, the other is the inscription, in runic letters, of the celebrated Ruthwell cross [9]). But all three taken together would furnish but scanty materials for a deeper study of the dialect in which they are written. The peculiarities of this would probably for ever have been unknown, had not the decay of learning among the Northumbrian clergy come to our help [1]). As the Latin became scanty, the Latin translations of the Bible and the La in rituals became unintelligible to many of the clerks, and it was found necessary so assist them by translations in the vernacular tongue. So the interlineary glosses came into existence [2]). Fortunately for us, four, or at least three, of these,

[6]) He seems to have been a bondsman. THORPE's Caedmon, p. XX.
[7]) — — ut quidquid ex divinis literis per interpretes disceret, hoc ipse post pusillum, verbis poëticis maxima suavitate et compunctione, in sua, id est Anglorum, lingua proferret.
    BEDA, quot. in THORPE's Caedmon p. XIX.
[8]) In Catal. M. S. S. Septent.
[9]) At Ruthwell, Dumfries'sh.
[1]) Be it, however, mentioned that Mr INNES, Scotl. in the M. Ages, p. 64, thinks, that it was better in this respect in Northumbria than in the southern provinces of England; the biographer of king Alfred not bestowing upon it the same censure of ignorance, which he lavishes on the latter. But it is difficult to see how a province, more than the south of England exposed to the inroads of the heathen Danes, could have better withstood the destruction.
[2]) That the glossators themselves not always were first-rate scholars, the glosses show to satiety; see f. i. BOUTERWEK's edition of the Lindisf. Gospels, Einleitung p. C.

written in the North-Anglic dialect, are still preserved, and in them we find materials for a study of this branch of the Old-English language [3]).

On reasons which cannot well be developed before the exposition of the North-Anglic dialect as it presents itself in M. S. S. which we know to have been written within its district, taking for granted that the interlineary gloss of the Cotton Psalter is not North-Anglic, at least in the strict sense of this word, we must take into consideration which of the remaining glosses possesses the greatest probability of giving a true specimen of the dialect in question. We have further to inquire into the time, when it was written, and the locality where the translator lived. The latter must have been in the heart of the district of the dialect; if the writer is known to have been a native of the locality, so much the better. — Of the three glosses known as the Lindisfarne-Gospels, the Durham Ritual, and the Rushworth Gospels, we know pretty well when the Ritual was interlined, the translator having taken care to inform his readers that at least a portion of the work was executed in A. D. 970, and GARNETT is of opinion that the whole may safely be referred to the same time and, as for its locality, to Durham or its vicinity [4]). As for the Lindisfarne-Gospels we are not so fortunate, but the general cast of orthography and the grammatical forms correspond so closely with those of the Ritual, that there cannot, reasonably, be the least doubt of their being also from the latter half of the 10th century, and from a locality where the dialect was the same as at Durham [5]).

---

[3]) Among the publications of the *Surtees Society*, to whose well-directed exertions the student of North-England's antiquities owes so much, is also found a volume entitled: The Latin Hymns of the A. S. Church with an interlinear A. S. gloss, ed. J. Stevenson. This gloss is not in the North-Anglic, but in W. S. dialect.

[4]) GARNETT, Philol. Essay's, p. 182. We cannot here enlarge upon any criticisms respecting the age of the M. S. S. in question. We follow the opinion current among English scholars: WANLEY, KEMBLE, Sir FR. MADDEN; and refer those who wish to know the objections that can be made to this opinion to the introduction prefixed to Mr BOUTERWEK's ed. of the Li. Gospels.

[5]) Mr BOUTERWEK (p. CVIII), from a comparison between the

The inspection of the Rushworth gloss puzzles us not a little. In the orthography it approaches much to the Ritual and the Lind. Gospels, but follows also in many points the common W. S. practice; while the grammatical forms in general closely correspond with the W. Saxon ones. From the latter circumstance to infer, that in this gloss we have the North-Anglic dialect at an earlier stage of development, would be very hazardous, it not being proved to be from the same locality as the Ritual. Besides, it does not agree with itself, but exhibits very marked discrepancies in its first and last portions. What we said of its aproximating to the W. S., concerns chiefly that part which was executed by Farmen, who stiles himself priest at Harawuda, a name which GARNETT thinks identical with Harewood in the West-Riding of Yorkshire. This conjecture accounts very well for the preponderance of W. S. forms, the mentioned place being situate on the southern border of the North-Anglic dialect, where this necessarily may have been much influenced by the midland tongue. — The latter portion of the gloss, executed by Owen, agrees with the Lindisfarne Gospels and the Ritual [6] — Here some questions of great difficulty present

---

Lindisf. Gospels, the Saxon Chronicle, and other monuments from the period of decay of the literary W. Saxon, regards the assigning of the former to the 12th century as necessary and unquestionable. His reasons, however, have little power with me, and I think it possible to show that just internal grounds, due allowance made for the ignorance of the glossators, speak for the high age of the language in the Ritual and the Lind. Gospels. — p. CII he says that the Rushworth codex presents "die Sprache auf einer etwas jüngeren Entwickelungsstufe." How has Mr B. found out that? On supposing, as Mr B., for aught I can see, really does, the W. S. forms to be the more ancient (a supposition hardly tenable, and leading to false conclusions with respect to the N. Anglic glosses) he ought also to consider the Rushworth codex, where the W. S. forms prevail, as more ancient than the Ritual and the Lindisfarne Gospels. — What we here have alluded to, will afterwards be discussed more closely, when the analysis of the North-Anglic has given a sufficiently broad basis for our operations.

[6]) Of the Rushworth gloss I have unfortunately only had the opportunity of perusing the Gospel of St. Matth., printed by STEVENSON, along with the same Gospel of the Lindisf. gloss. and part of the 4 ch, of the Gospel of St. John, printed by GARNETT, Philos. Essays, p. 184.

themselves. Are the two portions executed at the same time, or does a certain interval of time fall between the execution of the part of Farmen and that of Owen? Were both translators natives of the same country? — The decision of these questions would be of great interest to us. But we totally want dates for an answer to the latter, and the other, although the following analysis of the dialect, in some points at least, will give a clue to the case as it stands, we can no more hope to get satisfactorily answered.

As for the age of the Rushworth gloss, WANLEY [1]), whom GARNETT, subscribing his opinion, calls a good judge of the age of M. S. S., refers it to the end of the 9th, or the beginning of the 10th century.

We see, then, that the quality required in a literary monument in order to make its authority, in point of language, completely conclusive: to have been executed in the heart of the district where the dialect, in which it is written, was spoken, is only possessed by the Durham Ritual, and the Lindisfarne Gospels. In these, consequently, we have to take up our headquarters, and to this standard we have to refer the other monuments that claim a North-Anglic origin.

The very first glance at one of the North-Anglic M. S. S. shows the difference from the common W. S. in the spelling, on consequent there must also have been a difference of pronunciation. This we may presume; but that, I think, is all. As we ignore the real power of the complex vowels of the W. S., we cannot conceive what difference of pronunciation corresponded with the difference between the W. S. and the N. A. modes of spelling. In some cases the difference is, perhaps, more a seeming than a real one. Thus the frequent use of i in the N. A. where the W. S. has e may have constituted no real difference of pronunciation, it being tolerably certain that e in W. S., corresponding with the j of the Icel., was, before a following vowel, sounded as the y consonant of the present English. It is likely to suppose that the N. A. hiora, hio, hiorde etc. sounded very nearly as the W. S. heora, heo, heorde etc.

---

[1]) Quot. in Garnett's Philol. Essays, p. 183.

We must, further, take into consideration, that within the range of what we call West-Saxon (= Anglo-Saxon, as opposed to the North-Anglic) there existed no standard orthography, every author following his own method of spelling (if method there was at all), a circumstance which, as I have before alluded to, may be considered as depending, partly at least, on the W. S. itself being split into a multiplicity of subdivisions, differing in minutiæ, but yet differing enough to produce varieties of spelling. In consequence of this, it is no easy matter, for the sake of comparison, to fix a standard W. S. orthography, with which we can safely contrast the N. A. forms. We shall therefore, without any attempts at picking out all minutious differences which possibly may exist, confine ourselves to showing forth the more prominent features in which the North-Anglic vowelsystem appears to differ from that of the literary West-Saxon [8]).

Beginning with *a*, this vowel appears to have more often retained its purity in the N. A. than in the W. S. The *a* begins many words, that in the latter have *a* obscured by *e*, = *ea* [9]): all Li. Mr. 4, 34, Lu. 9, 9; aldor Li. Mt. 26, 59; arð Li. Mr. 14, 70; am Li. Mt. 11, 29; Lu. 21, 8; arm (brachium), arm (egenus) Bout. Gl. arg Li. Mt. 12, 39, Mr. 8. 38.

Sometimes this *a* has passed into *e* (= *é*?) ego Li. Mt. 6, 22; Mr. 9. 46, eher Li. Mt. 12, 1. Mr. 4, 28, eðelic Li. Mr. 10, 27, espryng Mr. 5, 29; erfeviardnisse Rit. p. 65.

The *ea* is however often preserved: ea Li. Mt. 7, 25; eadges Rit, p. 66; eardia Li. Mt. 13, 32; earn Li. Mt. 24, 28; earðe Li. Mr. 4, 31; easta Li. Lu. 13, 29; eaðe Li. Mr. 11, 13; eatta Li. Mt. 15: 20; meard Li. Mt. 10: 41; this is more

---

[8]) For a comparison of the vowelsystem of the N. A. with those of the other branches of the Teutonic tongue, the reader is referred to KEMBLE'S paper in the Proceedings of the Philological Society vol. II, p. 124. — The N. A. shows in its letters a close affinity to the O. Friesian. A comparison between them cannot here be instituted; the reader is referred to GRIMM, D. Gr. I. pp. 269—280.

[9]) I give here only a circumscribed number of instances, as more will be found in the subsequent exposition of the grammatical peculiarities; nor do I quote all passages in which the here given words occur.

particularly the case in the former part of the Rushworth gloss. There is however in the N. A. monuments great vacillation in the use of *ea, a, e*, and the one is often put instead of the other, quite as we find it in the W. S.:

hearta Rit. p. 5, 1; herte Li. Lu. 8, 14 eatta; eta Li. Mt. 11, 18; earm Rit. p. 92, 2; arm (v. above).

In the midst of the words *ea* is retained; ceastre Rit. p. 65; gelearnade Li. Mt. 2, 7, stearres Li. Mt. 2, 7; fearr Li. Mr. 12, 1; deaf Li. Mr. 7, 32; dead Li. Mr. 6, 22, Rit. p. 27; steap-cildo Rit. p, 29, 31; gefealla Li. Lu. 2, 36; but it is also changed into *e:* dernelegere Li. Mt. 19, 9; cester Li. Mt. 9, 35; heh Li. Lu. 1, 78; or *a:* halda Li. Mr. 14, 44; halt Li. Mt. 11, 5; halmas Li. Mt. 3, 12; halfe Li. Mr. 1, 45; harmcuode Li. Lu. 6, 28; ich darr Bout. p. 267. Of *a* standing for W. S. *e* in the gen. pl. of nouns of the simple order, instances will be given under these nouns.

a is, further, often found in the particip., pres. and past, of the weak verbs instead of the W. S. *e* and *o,* and in the pret. of verbs belonging to Rask's 1, 1, where it also supplies the latter vowel. The inspection of the Mœso-Gothic informs us, that the N. A. forms must be the more ancient.

Examples [1]):

bodande Mr. 1, 39, Lu. 20, 1; milsande Mr. 1, 41; 5, 19, hrinande Mr. 1, 41; gebiddande Mt. 26, 39; geecnande Lu. 1, 31, falletande Mr. 5, 5; smeande Mr. 2, 6; gestiorande Mr. 11, 24; foreondetande Lu, 2, 3; œfistande Lu. 2, 16; gebloedsando Lu. 24, 53; lufiande Lu. 6, 32.

gebloedsad Lu. 1, 28; gefotad Mr. 15, 44; forebodad Mt. 24, 14; genið̆rad Mt. 27, 3; gesomnad Mt. 28, 12; unavidlades Rit. p. 24, 2; gihalgad Rit. p. 65; gesomnade Rush. Mt. 25, 32; geclaensad Mr. 1: 42, gecostad Lu. 12, 56.

ofeliopade Mr. 15, 34; gefraegnade, geascade Mr. 15: 2; bodadon Mr. 16, 20; awundradon. Lu. 1, 21; hlattade ihm; ðerhwunade Luc. 1, 21; fearrade Lu. 1, 38; gesuigade Lu. 18, 39; micJade Lu. 18, 43; losade Lu. 19, 10; gisyngades Rit.

---

[1]) From Li. when not marked otherwise.

p. 11: 14; gesomnade Rush. Mt. 2, 4; slepade Rush. Mt. 25, 5; geginade J. 16, 24; geberhtnade J. 14, 32; geendade Mt. 11, 1. I think it superfluous to give examples of *a*, in all three cases, being changed into *o* (*u*), or *e*, as those are the common W. S. forms.

Sometimes, although upon the whole seldom, *a* appears instead of *i*: in the oblique cases of the pron ðes, ðios, ðis: anum ðassa metdmaasta Li. Mt. 25, 45; ðassum monnum Li. Mr. 14, 60; ðassum here Li. Lu. 9, 13; ðasum wordum Li. Lu. 9, 28; on ðasser naeht Li. Mt. 26, 31; for ðidder, we find, Li. J. 7, 35, ðadder; and in a few verbs, of which the most remarkable is wallas (or wallað) Li. Mt. 12, 38, and very often. When ne is prefixed, it generally changes into *a*, or *ae*, but is sometimes preserved: nallas Li. Mt. 6, 7; naellas ibm 5, 17; nellað ibm 7, 1.

In the same way *ae* takes the place of W. S. *i*: naeht Li. Mt. 4, 2, etc. maeht Li. Mt. 7, 29 etc. enaeht Li. Mt. 2, 8, 9. maehton ibm 17, 16. — Before leaving *a*, we must mention the practice of inserting it after a preceding *e*: cearro Li. Mt. 12, 44; gefreates Li. Mt. 6, 19; to geafanne Bout. p. 279, 9; wealigo. Li. Mr. 12, 41; to geðearseanne Li. Mr. 15, 15. These examples are, however, not frequent. That *o* sometimes supplies its place, is, the continual interchange between these two vowels in the N. A. considered [2]), a matter of course. — There might be said a good deal about the obscuration of *a*, and its transition into the cognate simple or complex vowel-sounds, but, as we here only can sketch some outlines of the N. A. vowel-system, we must leave these more nice discursions.

e stands for W. S. *eo*: leht Li. Mt. 17, 5, and for W. S. *ae*: efter Li. Mt. 24, 29; ellðiodig Li. Mt. 17, 26. merðu

---

[2]) So we sometimes find a for o = um: of ðissa Li. J. 14, 7; from ðissa ic iuh cuoeðo ibm, 13, 19; se faeder wyrcað from ðissa, ibm 5, 17. — I beg to refer the reader to what is said concerning the cases required by these two prepositions, p. 25, in the note; but it is obvious that from ðissa is with more reason considered as an apocopated dat. than as the neut. acc. ðis with a vowel affixed in the way shown a little further down.

Li. Mr. 1, 28. These variations, however, are not constant, and, therefore, not much stress is to be laid on them.[3])

More characteristic for the N. A. than this substitution of the slender e for W. S. eo, and ae, is the pretty regular substitution of the obscure vowel-combination oe for the broad e (= é) of the W. S.[4]).

Examples:

gefoerde Li. Mt. 15, 21, 22; cuoeðende ibm 15, 22; ofdoeme Li Mt. 16, 3; soecas ibm 16, 4; woenað Li. Lu. 13, 4; boene Rit. p. 40, 6; gifoestnigað ibm; ymbwoend ibm; voeron Rit. 44, 5; woerig Rush. J. 4. qu. GARN. (In the Rush. Gospel of St. Matth. oe does *not* occur.) doege Li. J. 4, 45; avoecco Li. J. 11, 11; gefoerum ibm 11, 16; gewoedum Li. Mr. 15, 20; ahloefa Rit. p. 55, 3; huoerf Li. Lu. 6, 35. It must be mentioned, that although the practice is upon the whole, well kept up, e often is found for oe; so the last word occurs, Li. Lu. 6, 34, twice written huerf.

i stands often for W. S. e. As we afterwards shall have

---

[3]) As for the dropping of e, originated in one way or another, and which is no peculiarity of the N. A., cf. Bout. p. CXXIV. — Of the superfluously affixed e we shall speak afterwards.

[4]) GARNETT, Philol. Essays p. 180, observes, that "the analogy of the cognate dialects shows, that the Anglian are the more original forms:" but it is impossible not to subscribe to the objection of Dr. LATHAM, Hndbk of the Eng. Langu. (4 ed.) p. 137, that, as we are ignorant of the real power of the W. S. é, "the difference of pronunciation is, by no means, so clear as the difference of spelling." This objection is backed by the orthography of the Ruthwell Runes, where we find the simple e for the oe of the Glosses: limwêrigne Ruth.; woerig Li. J. 4, 6; estig Ruth., oestig Rit. p. 30, 7; bismerede and geredae Ruth., ought, from analogy, in the glosses to have been: bismoerede and geroedae, but are written: bismeredon Li. Mt. 27, 29, geraeda Rit. p. 86, 2. — Perhaps, then, was the oe of the glosses a peculiarity confined to a limited district of the region, within which the N. A. dialect was current. It may at least, as will be shown, when we come to treat of this dialect on a stage of farther development, be presumed, that there existed other branches of it than that one preserved in the Lindisfarne Gospels, the Durham Ritual, and the last portion of the Rushworth Gospels.

occasion to give an account of its use in the verbal forms, we here only give instances of its occurring in nouns. oðri ðegnas Li. J. 21, 8; gloedi voeron ibm v. 9; ðiu segni ibm v. 11; ðaem biscobi Li. J. 18, 22 (biscobe v. 24), sio Li. J. 18. 17; ðaem caseri Li. Mt. 22, 17; ðerh syndrigi Li. J. 21, 25; ðiddir ibm v. 18; hio. Of *o* we remark the continual interchange with *u* and, sometimes with *a* [5]) and *e* — examples in the following. — The practice of inserting it after a preceding *i*, without any reasonable ground, must be particularly mentioned, as it constitutes a peculiarity of N. A. orthography.

Examples:

lioniandra Li. J. 13, 28 and often; ðiosne Rush. J. 4. Garn.; Rit. p. 188; Li. J. 9, 39; ðios (= ðis?) Li. 4, 39, 40; gegrioppo Li. J. 7, 32: scioppo Li. J. 6. 23, 24; hrioppað Li. J. 4, 37; wrioto Li. Mt. 26, 56; fordriofon Li. J. 9, 34; stioredon Li. Mr. 10, 13: niomas Li. Mr. 16, 18, arioson Rit. p. 43, 2; Li. Mt. 25, 7; tlioton Li. J. 9, 22; liofo Li. J. 6, 57, 58; bioðon Li. Lu. 21, 11; sciolon ibm 13, 5. Most of these words are, however, also found without the inserted *o*:

hlinigað Li. Lu. 13, 29; scilon Li. Mr. 14, 62; biðon Li. Lu. 21, 24; gegripa Rit. p. 5; scip Li. Mr. 1, 19, 20; writto Li. Mr. 14, 20; writto Li. Mr, 14, 49; ic hrippo Li. Mt. 25, 26; fordrifa Li. Mt. 12, 20; nimeð Li. J, 1, 29; hlifige Li. Mr. 5, 23; arisson Li. Lu, 24, 33. Many more instances, of the one kind as well as of the other, might easily be compiled. I think, however, that those already produced suffice for deciding the question: was the *o*, inserted in the said manner, sounded in the pronunciation? ·in a negative way. For such a conclusion plead not only the forms, where it is left out, but also the whole subsequent development of the dialect. Had its insertion been anything more than a fancy of the glossators [6]),

---

[5]) Also in the gen. pl.: Zebedeis Suno moder Li. Mt. 20, 20.

[6]) Was, perhaps, o behind i, as a after e (see above), inserted to note the length of the preceding vowel? A glance at the examples shows sufficiently, that this question can the one time be answered in the affirmative, the other in the negative.

traces enough would, in all probability, have remained in the N. A. of the Middle-Ages. — Concerning the consonants we will set forth only those facts which we consider most characteristic, and most interesting in our point of view. Our remarks, then, will be exclusively confined to the three consonants *n*, *t*, and *w* [7]).

The casting off of the *n* in the simple order of nouns will afterwards be spoken of. — In general there is in the N. A. a strong tendency towards its dropping. and it may take place wherever a word whatever terminates in *n* behind a vowel, particularly when this vowel is *a*, or *o*. Such is the case in the pres. subj. pl., pret. pl. indic. and subj., and the infin.; (examples under the verbs). In the same way numerals, and particles, in the W. S. terminating in *n*, are stript of the consonant:

(numerals) boege Li. Lu, 1, 7; 5, 39; tuoege Li. Lu. 15, 11; 22, 38; seofo Li. Lu. 2, 36; (particles) ðono Li. J. 9, 1, huono Li. J. 2, 9; Rit. p. 192; begonda Li. J. 1, 28; binna Li. J. 18, 15; easta, woesta, norda. suða Li. Lu. 13, 29; fearra Li. Lu, 22, 54; buta Li Lu. 13, 3; onufa Li. Lu, 15, 20; heona Li. Lu. 13, 31.

t stands sometimes for *d* in the past participle: bilyrtet Li. Mt. 2, 16; gecostat Li. St. Mt. 4, 1; gelaedet Li. Lu. 23, 32; gewoendet Li. Lu. 17, 4; gemoetet Lu. 17, 18; geendat Li. Lu. 22, 22; gesetlet Li. Lu. 23, 53; gesendet J. 1, 6; asendet J. 1, 24; getractat J. 9, 7. In nouns it occurs so seldom, that I think the few instances I have picked up not worth noticing.

w is sometimes dropt before *n*, *o*, and *y* [8]):

ulfum Li. Lu. 10, 3; ulf J. 10, 2; nðuttum Mt. 16, 21; 24, 27; uldre J. 11, 4; geunade J. 11, 6; geuna J. 14, 6; Lu. 4, 16; unas J. 1, 38; unade J. 11, 54; eueum Mt. 17, 44;

---

[7]) For other facts relative to the N. A. consonants, see Bouter. pp. CXXXVI—CLIV.

[8]) This is sometimes also the case in the O. Friesian; see RASK, Frisische Sprachlehre, übersetzt von Dr. F. J. Buss, p. 27; p. 36 RASK, from some other considerations, infers that the v, although left out in the spelling, was always sounded in the pronunciation.

coða Mt. 17, 20; cocrustan Mt. 18, 6; coen Lu. 11, 31; coern Mr. 9, 41; coeðas Mt. 23, 3; 26, 41; soefen Mt. 27, 19; hulco, hulic Mr. 13, 1; ymbhyrfe Luc. 2, 1; aundrad Luc. 7, 9; aðoa J. 13, 8, 10, 14. But, on the other hand, *w* is not seldom, quite gratuitously, put before the above-mentioned vowels: wutmestum Li. Mt. 25, 30; ðerhwurnon Mr. 7, 55; wuduutum Mr. 10, 33; 14, 53; ða wyflo Lu. 16, 25; gewunrotsað Lu. 18, 23. For more examples, see Bouterw. p. CXXXV.

Passing to the grammatical forms, we shall begin with the declensions of substantives, following the order adopted by Rask. The simple order presents this scheme [9]):

Singular	Plural
N. a, o, u, e (ae)	a, o (u)
G. a, o, u, e	ana (ena)
D. a, o, u, e	um, om
A. a, o, u, e	a, o, e (ae).

Examples:

ðaem noma waes Li. J. 1, 6; þte se witgae Li. Lu. 9, 8; sie willo ðin Li. Mt. 6, 10; monnum godes willo Li. Lu. 2, 14; is acasa geseted Li. Lu. 3, 9; ðios widiua Li. Lu. 2, 37; bethlem eorðu judæ Li. Mt. 2, 6; þu corðu Rush. Mt. 2, 6; ðin geleafo Li. Lu. 7, 50; ðio waes portcuoene Li. Lu. 7, 37; is mara witge Li. Lu. 7, 28; ðaes witgo Li. Mt. 12, 39; ne (se) gie gemende — — iwere(s) lichoma Li. Mt. 6, 25; (ge) lytle(s) geleafa (modicæ fidei) Li. Mt. 8, 26; from hearta monigfaldnisse Li. Mt. 12, 34; from eorðo gemaerum Li. Mt. 12, 42; mid user lichome bisene (cum nostræ carnis substantia) Rit. p. 4, 2; salt eorðu Bout. p. 279; after aes gewuna Li. Lu. 2, 27, 42; in hire hearta Li. Lu. 2, 51; on alle eorðo Li. Lu. 4, 25; from corðo Li. Lu. 5, 3; on corðu Li. J. 8, 8; in ege ðinum Rush. Mt. 7, 3; lichome (corpore) Rit. p. 40, 4; in —

---

[9]) The terminations of the nom. sg. have no reference to the gender of nouns; see the examples.

herte Li. Lu. 8, 15: ðerh ðone witgo Li. Mt. 2, 5, and often; gesegon -- steorra Rush. Mt. 2. 2. (Li. stearra); ðerh ðone witge Li. Mt. 2, 17, and often; cirica he getimbrade Li. Lu, 7, 5; þurh witgu Rush. Mt. 2, 15; gang in gefea ibdm 25, 21, 23; ne fund ic — — ðus micelo geleafo Li. Lu. 7, 9; erendwreco fromfoerdon Li. Lu. 7, 24; sie inero sido foregegyrdedo Li. Lu. 4. 25; inera noma sint Li. Lu. 10, 21; ðara witgana Li. Lu. 11, 47, 50; uðuutana Li. Lu. 20, 38; widuana l. widuena Li. Lu. 20, 47; allum witgom Li. Lu. 24, 27; uitgum Li. J, 1, 45; in iuerum heortum Li. Lu. 21. 14; on corðum ibm 21, 25; ðu ða witge afslaest ibm, 14, 34; ða ego —· ahebba ibm 18, 13; to undoenne — — (ða) witgae Li. Mt. 5, 17; cleafað hearta inero Rit. p. 5, 1, and p. 19, 12; hiora ega ahofon Li. Mt. 17, 8.

Provisionally supposing, that this declension has grown out of the simple W. S., we have only given such words as in the latter dialect follow the weak scheme. It is now to be shown, that in the N. A. it had a much wider range, and comprised not only the weak nouns of the W. S., but even all classes of RASK's complex order, except those forming their gen sg. in-es and nom pl. in-as, so that, strictly speaking, the N. A. possessed only two declensions: the one in all cases, except the dat. pl. [1]), ending in vowels, the other forming the gen. sg. in-es, and tqe nom. pl. in-as [2]). But it will also be seen, that not even

---

[1]) Sometimes, however, we fall in with dat. pl. having lost their-m, but I think that these instances are best considered as slips of the pen.

[2]) It would, perhaps, be more to the point to divide the N. A. nouns into three declensions:

1. nouns ending in nom. sg. in an essential a, o, u, or e, in gen. pl. in ana;

II. nouns ending in the gen. sg. in-es, in the nom. pl. like nom. sg., or taking an unessential vowel;

III. nouns forming their gen. sg. in-es, the nom. pl. in-as.

But beside these declensions we should have a good number of anomalies, as will soon be shown. The N. A. nouns seem in reality to laugh every attempt of classifying them to scorn; and to that one made just now many objections might easily be pointed out, were it not for our believing criticisms to be here quite out of place.

these two declensions were rigourously kept asunder, the one continually encroaching upon the purlieu of the other.

We begin with pointing out the manner in which the nouns of the compl. order were made to follow the vowel-declension, by adding an unessential vowel, changing the preexisting ones, and taking the gen. pl. in-ana, or-ena. It will be observed, that nouns of all three genders were alike subject to these changes.

Examples:

ðio biseno Li. Lu. 8, 9, 11; bið micelo ofersuiðnisso Li. Lu. 21, 23; min cydnisse ne is soð Li. J. 5, 31; waes oferawritteno inawritten Li. Lu. 23, 38; daege waes aworden Li. Lu. 22. 66; eadgo symbeltide (beata sollemnitas) Rit p. 53; monna wittnessa is Li. J. 8, 17; f'beadende—gaefelo to scallane l. þtese gesald Li. Lu. 23, 2; ðiosne monno ibm 23, 14, and often; hiora breosto slaegendo ibm 23, 48; ða wifo ibm 23, 55, and often; beron ða sueti stenco ibm 24, 1; gesaeh ða linen hraegla ibm 24, 12; ðas wordo ibm 24, 17; ne haefeð bano ibm 24, 39; sex uintro Li. J, 2, 20; his beeno ða ibm 2, 23; Godes sunu stefn Li. J. 5, 25; in min lufu Li. J, 15, 9; in-lufa, in his lufo ibm v. 10. ðas taceno ibm 3, 2; hiora uerco neron ibm 3, 19; ueron menigo uaetro ibm 3, 23; ðá brydo ibm, 3, 29; feuero monedo Li. J. 4, 35; ðe sune wyrcas Li. J. 5, 19; ðone sunu ibm 5, 20; worda mino Rit. p. 55, 3; usero fadero Li. J. 6, 31; ðaera palmana ³) Li. J. 12, 13; hlafana Li. Mt. 16, 9; fiscana Li. Lu. 5, 6, 9; ðeafana Li. Mr. 11, 17; warana Li. Lu. 14. 24; dagana ibm 5, 17; windana Rit. p. 192; sunana Bout. p. CLXIII; gimungana Rit. p. 108; wyrtana Rit. p. 3, 4; dingana Li. Lu. 1, 1; cildena Rit. p. 104 ⁴).

---

³) As a matter of course, it need scarcely be mentioned, that the regular gen. pl. in-a also occurs, and, in general, more frequently than those in-ana.

⁴) Mr BOUTERWEK, Die 4 Evang. in A. N. Humbr. Sprache, p. CLXIII, has picked up a number of N. A. forms, which, he thinks, show that the dat. sg. in-a of the W. S. winter, duru etc. had a wider range in the former dialect than in the latter. But it is evident, that most of them may as well be considered as gen., or accus., the prepositions from which Mr. B. concludes the presence of a dat. in the N. A. also

The preceding examples, easily to be multiplied, show, we are of opinion, sufficiently the tendency of the N. A. to substitute *o* for *e* (= originally *a?* as *e* generally seems to be the last stage of the transmutation of vowels, when the are going to be dropt); to affix a vowel, commonly *o*, but sometimes *a* or *e*, to words terminating in consonants, particularly, as it appears, when these consonants are liquids, or the spirans *s*; to transfer the pl. termination-as into *o*, and, finally, to give nouns of the complex order the gen. pl. in-ana.

But had the vowel-declension made encroachment upon the territory of the complex order, and transformed into wavering subjects some of its citizens, we shall soon be aware, that the latter did not fail to take its revenge, and in the 10th century already had begun those proceedings that ended in making him so completely victorious over his rival, that, in our days, only a very few of the subjects of his survive, after having escaped the destruction of their brethren, or their being put into the ranks of the hostile army [5]).

We shall, then, review the recruits of the declension forming the gen. sg. in-es and the nom. pl. in-as, and begin with those in the W. S. belonging to the simple order of Rask.

Examples:

ðaes witges Li. St. prol. p. 12, l. 21; tið stearres Li. Mt. 2, 7; salt eorðes Li. Mt. 5, 13; his lichomes Li. J. 2, 21;

---

governing these cases: from hia Li. Mr. 16, 11; from synna hiora Li. St. Mt. 1, 21 (Mr B. has from hiora synnum); fro hehsynno usra Rit. p. 42; of ocles cowres Rush. Mt. 25, 8; so that, in many instances, it is impossible to make out what case they in reality govern. The difficulty is, besides, increased, by the great incertainty that prevails in the use of the vowels, the same word, in the same case, often terminating in three or four different ways.

[5]) In the W. S., which stubbornly stuck to the final-n, and only late gave it up, the struggle was better poised on the part of the simple order. To judge from the language of some of the South-English middle-age-romances, it might even seem, that it had won a few advantages over the "strong" enemy. — The greatest plenty of uncommon plurals in-en I ever found in any of the books alluded to, is in Arthur and Merlin (Edinburgh, 1838, 4:o), where the very devil (l. 665) has become "simple."

brydgumes Li. Lu. 5, 34; his tunges Li. Mr. 7, 35; heartes Li. Mr. 10, 5, geleafas Li. Lu. 12, 28; ða steorras hcofnes Li. Mr. 13, 25; tuoge culfras birdas Li. Lu. 2, 24. — These, I think, are all; but each of them is often fallen in with.

We now give some examples of feminines of Rask's II, 3 having been drawn under the same declension, and turn at the same time the reader's attention to the change of gender, which appears often to have followed the change of declension [6]).

ða costunges dagas Li. Mr. 13, 18; ðaem ebolsong Li. J. 10, 33; cossetunges Li. Lu. 7, 45; gitsungas, efolsongas ibm 7, 22; foresceaunges Rit. p. 38; ðines groetenges Li. Lu, 1., 44; ðaes of'suiðung Li. J. 16, 21; smeaungas Li Lu. 24, 38; teigðunegas ibm 18, 12; fiunges ibm 14, 26; fadorlices giselenisses Rit. p. 24; soðfaestnises gaast Li. J. 15, 26; ðaes hefignise ibm 16, 12; ðis smirinise ibm 12, 5; gemnisses Li. Mr. 3, 15; hreownises Li. Mr. 1, 4; lustgiornisses ibm 4, 19. The nouns in-is are never found to form their pl. in-as.

maehtes ðines Rit. p. 51; cennices rest ibm p. 66, 3; ðinum milsac ibm p. 42, 18; haeses Li. Lu. 3, 1; lufes Rit. p. 126, 8; helles Li. Mt. 16, 18; rodes Rit. p. 21.3; stefne miclum Rit. p. 44, and often in Li.; his saules Li. Mr. 8, 36. — The following fem. nouns follow in the W. S. the III, 3 of Rask:

haeles Li. Lu. 1, 77; gefes Rit. p. 17, 22; snyttres Rit. p. 120, 1.

For the sake of completeness, the following forms, not comprised in any of the preceding categories, may also be given:

sunes Bout. p. 277; moderes Li. Lu. 1, 15; and often; broðres ðines Li. Mt. 7, 3; fiondas Li. Mt. 5, 44, and often; freondas ibm 23, 30, and often.

As examples of nouns of the neuter gender passing into the masc. declension, it may be enough to quote:

---

[6]) Change of gender is also found to have taken place on such nouns as heorta etc. being drawn under the mascul. declension: iueres heartes Li. Mr. 10, 5: on godum corðo ibm 4, 8; etc. Upon the whole, a great confusion reigns in respect to gender. — It need not be mentioned, that the nouns in-ung, -is etc. also occur as femin.

holas Li. Mt. 8. 20; ricas middangeardes ibm 4, 8; nestasl nestu ibm 8, 20.

Before leaving the nouns we must notice some few remains of a pl. in-r:

foed mino lombor Li. J. 21, 15; mino lomboro [7]) ibm 16; sua lambra Li. Lu. 10, 2: aefter tuaem dogrum l dagum Li. Mt. 26, 2; aefter twaem dogrum Li. Mr. 14. 1; ðerh ðreo dogor ibm 14, 58; (hia) — ðriodogor mec geanbidas ibm 8, 2. As the inquiry of these forms is better deferred until later, we here confine ourselves to pointing out, as somewhat extraordinary-looking, the *o* in dogrum, daeg in the N. A. always observing the W. S. practice to replace *a* before an *a* or a *u* of the following syllable. —

The N. A. adjectives have, in every point, shared in the changes which the N. A. nouns have undergone, and we meet there the same confusion of gender. The definite inflection of the adjectives, closely agreeing with the simple order of nouns, has dropt the final *n*, and shows the same uncertainty in the use of vowels, *o*, *u*, or *e*, the last often left out, being substituted for *a*. Under such circumstances, — the indefinite declension also having undergone considerable curtailing in the terminations: the -um of the dat. masc. and neut. frequently softened into *e*, which often is dropt, and the *n* of the acc. masc. and *r* of gen. and dat. fem. having followed the same way, the two declensions had become nearly alike, — it may easily be fancied, that a confusion must take place, and that it was impossible any more to keep the two declensions separate. This, indeed, we also find. The following examples will show 1) the N. A. forms of the defin. declens. of adject.: 2) the promiscuous use of defin. declension for indefin., and vice versa: 3) adjectives of one gender determining subst. nouns of another [8]).

gebaer sunu þone frumkendu Rush. Mt. 1, 24 : — — hire frumcende Li. ibm; geccigde (þa) tungulcraeftga Li. Mt. 2, 7; tungulkraeftigu quomon Rush. Mt. 2, 1; þene unnytte esne Rush. Mt. 25, 30; ne cunnade ða ileo Li. Mt. 1, 24; fleita ða ilea

---

[7]) O affixed conformably to the practice mentioned above.

[8]) We think it superfluous to give any examples of the occurrence of regular forms of the defin. as well as of the indefin. declension.

ibm 7, 19; ymb ðy ðirrda tid ibm 20, 3; ðone neste Rit. p. 65; ðaes heista witga Li. Lu. 1, 76; ðaes heiste Li. Lu. 6, 35. (hia) ða untrymigo gelecnadun Li. Lu. 9, 1; on ðacm hlaettmesta daege Li. J. 11, 24; ðaem blinde Li. J. 9, 17. — Se welig Li. Mr. 10, 25; þ god uin Li J. 2, 10; — ðaes wloncas Li. Lu. 16. 21; ðaes blindaes hond Li. Mr. 8, 23; ðaes blindborenes ego Li. J. 9, 32; his halges cydnisse Li. Lu. 1, 72; ðe halges Godes Rit. p. 66, 3; haeles blindas and halte Li. St. prol. p. 33, 27. — eadges Marie Rit. p. 66. Some other instances might be quoted, but they are more dubious, the fem. nouns in -is, -ung, etc. often being used as masc. —

The peculiarities of the N. A. pronouns seem chiefly to consist in the spelling, *i* being put instead of the W. S. *e*, and *u* often inserted behind a preceding *i*, or *c*. — Deferring to quote passages where they occur, until we shall have to treat of the N. A. forms of the verbs, we here only give those forms of the pronouns which seem worth noticing.

I. Ic; dat. and acc. sg. mec, meh, mech, me; dual. acc. ungket, Ruthw. Cross [9]); pl. vc. uoe, woe; dat. and acc. usih, us.

II. ðu; dat. and acc. sg. ðec, ðech, ðeh, ðe; pl. ge, gie; gen. iuerro; dat. and ac. iuh. iuih, iwih.

III. The declension of he, hio, (hiu), hit, has nothing particular, except the insertion of *o* (*a*) already alluded to. Hio is in acc. sg. hio or hea. The common pl. is: n. hia, g. hiora, d. him (heom), a. hia (hiu).

The declens. and use of the demonstratives exhibit some remarkable peculiarities. The W. S þaet, se, seo, is, as in the O. Friesian, rather þact, þe, þio (ðiu); se occurs not seldom, but seo has nearly grown out of use. [1]). In the inflection only the acc. sg. ðy, for ðone and ða, calls for attention [2]):

---

[9]) GRIMM, Deutsche Gramm. I. (2 ed). p. 781, had already supposed this dualform, in analogy with the acc. dual. incit.

[1]) sio is only found in the Li. Gospel of St. John: sio tid 1, 39; 4, 23: 5, 28; sio ðignen 18, 17; sio menigo 12, 12. This fact, I think, speaks for the opinion of Mr Bouterwek (p. XLVII), that the glossator of this gospel is not the same as the glossator of the three other gospels, in which sio never occurs.

[2]) sometimes ðy is for ðio: — ceastra ðy is genemned Li. Mt. 2, 23.

.— on daege ðy 1 ðe (he) ne hyhtað Li. Lu. 12, 46; steorra ðy (hia) gesegon Li. Mt. 2, 9; se drithen ðy (quam) gesege Li. Lu. 7, 13. These forms, however, are of a very rare occurrence, and I am inclined to see in them only a misspelling of the indeclinable ðe. For this speaks its very extensive use in the N. A., where it often supplies the inflected article se in the nom. sg. [3]), and even, now and then, is found dispossessing it in the oblique cases.

Examples:

ðe Haelend Li. Mr. 3, 7; and often; ðe diowl ibm v. 23; ðe widerword ibm v. 23; geherde Herodes ðe kyng Li. St. Mt. 2, 3; aras ðe sacerda aldor Li Mt. 26, 62; ðe ambeht Li. J. 21, 23; ðe halges godes sunu cennices rest. Rit. p. 66, 3; ðe cynig Herodes sunu Li. Mt. 2, 22; þurh Esaiam þe witgu Rush. Mt. 1, 22; ðe ðirddan daeg eftarisa Li Mt. 16, 21; lufa ðin ðe neste Li. Lu. 10. 27. — I think, however, that too great stress ought not to be laid on the last six examples, and that they, perhaps, best are considered as slips of the pen. — More interesting is another application of this pronoun, as it seems to have contributed not a little to bring about the change in consequence of which the present English wants a plural of he, and a nom. sg. of her. The determ. pronoun serves, indeed, already in the Rit. and Li. as a surrogate for he, hio, hit, and

---

[3]) GRIMM, D. Gram. I. p. 391, is of opinion, that se and seo are of another origin than the forms used as their oblique cases, and that þe and þeo in the A. S. are of a more recent date. It is true, that in the Moeso-Goth. we have sa corresponding to se, and sô to seo; and in the Old-Norse sa = A. S. se, and sû = A. S. seo, but in the O. High-Germ, O. Saxon, and O. Friesian, the masc. and fem. are of the same root as the neut. and the oblique cases. If we suppose þ in the A. S. þe and þeo to have had the sharp sound of th in think, the transition of þ into s is, I think, easily accounted for, and the necessity of supposing different roots for se and þe disappears. Examples of this transition are not wanting; and there is, I think, still in the English a certain tendency to change þ into s, and ð into d. — But why was þ preserved in the neut. þaet, and in the oblique cases? — Languages are sometimes very capricious!

not seldom the glossators seem to have hesitated, if they should use forms of the one or the other [4]).

Examples:

ðas hine sprecende to him 1 ðaem Li. Mt. 9, 18; geleenade hea 1 ða Li. Mt. 15, 30; hia 1 ða saegdon ibm 2, 5; in ðaer 1 in ðaem acenned is ibm 1, 20; cegde esnas his and salde þaem his god Rush. Mt. 25, 14; gilef þte ðere (?) symbel' ne bigaað ðerh ðaes to ðe biseno gistepe ve Rit. p. 51; from him 1 ðaem (hia) micel bebodadon — of ðaem hia mara willniað Li. Lu. 12, 48; nacod (he) from ðaem foreflach Li. Mr. 14, 52; brengað ðene hidir to me Li. Mt. 17, 17; and hiora 1 ðara gecydnise ne waes woenlic Li. Mr. 14, 59; his 1 ðaes onsion naes Li. J. 11, 44; fifo of ðaem weron Li. Mt. 25, 2.

The remainder of the N. A. pronouns, and the numerals, exhibiting no peculiarities, except those of spelling, we pass on to the *Verbs*. The strong ones of these do not command any particular attention [5]). We will only, en passant, make the remark, that I have not been able to find the slightest trace of vowelchange (Umlaut) in pret. subjunct., and the 2 pers. sg. pret. indic. [6]), and that, consequently, the O. Norse strong conjugation has not stamped its mark upon them. It may be that they differ in some insignificant points from the forms exhibited by

---

[4]) RASK, Frisische Sprachlehre, §. 118, remarks, that the demonst. pron. is in the O. Friesian often used in the same way.

[5]) The following verbal forms, showing a decline of the complex order, and tendency to pass over into the simple order, deserve a particular notice:

astigade Li. Lu. 10, 30; stagade Li. J. 5, 4 (the first a = i) ingeberigde 1 ingebarg Li. J. 2, 9; geðringed Li. Lu. 8, 42; gedringdon Li. Mr. 5, 24; gebegd(on) Li. Mt. 27, 29; Mr. 10, 17; gebeged Li. Lu. 18, 14; Mt. 23, 12; gesninged Li. Mr. 12, 9; Lu. 12, 47; gesaudes Li. Lu. 19, 21; ofergeseaw 1 gesecawde Mt. 13, 25; slepade Rush. Mt. 25, 5; geslepdon Li. ibm; gegrippde Li. Lu. 9, 39; gegrippedon Li. Lu. 23, 26; gegraeppadon (ae = i) Li. Mt. 14, 31; gehrinade Li. Lu. 18, 15; Mt. 14, 36; gefraegnade Li. Mr. 15, 2, and often; geserenede Li. Mt. 13, 7; woepde(n) Li. Lu. 7, 32.

[6]) see GRIMM, D. Gr. I. p. 901.

the standard W. S., but these differences are best referred to the idiomatic peculiarities of the N. A. vowelsystem [7]).

Our remarks, then, will exclusively bear upon the weak verbs; but we must first make an account of the substant. ones. Wosa (W. S. wesan) is in pres. ind. sg. am, arð, is; pl. aron, aron, aron [8]):

Ic am soð wintreo, and min faeder is londbuend Li. J. 15, 1; arð ðu se ðe tocymende is Li. Mt. 11, 3; arð ðu Judeane cynig? Li. Mr. 15, 2; ic am Li. J. 18, 6; huaed arst 1 arð ðu Li. J. 1,19; suae ue aron an Li. J. 17, 22, 28; gileseno aron gie Rit. p. 24, hogað gie no ða ðe of' eorðe aron Rit. p. 25; iweres heafdes hero aron getalad Li. Lu. 12, 7.

The subjunctive is se or sie, in sg. and pl.:

þte min hus se gefylled Li. Lu. 15, 23; þte (ðiu) lufo sie Li. J. 17, 26; ge ne se besuicen Li. Lu. 21, 8; þte (hia) sie an Li. J. 17, 21.

Among the forms of beon, N. A. bian, Li. Mt. 1, 20, (I am not aware of a bia), we remark the 1 pres. ind. sg. beom, or biom, and the pl. biðon (bioðon). The subjunct., bie or bia, appears to be nearly out of use, it is at least seldom met with [9]): ic beom hal 1 gehaeled ic biom Li. Mr. 5, 28; ic am 1 ic beom L. J. 12, 26; gie biðon [deado] Li. J. 8, 21, biðon geondspurnad Li. Mr. 4, 17; bioðon Li. Mt. 11, 8, and often; bie 1 se allra ðrael Li. Mr. 10, 44; sie 1 bia iur ðea Li. Mt. 20, 27.

The first peculiarity of the regular verbs [1]) calling for attention is 1 pres. ind. in —m, once transformed into —n.

---

[7]) GRIMM, Gesch. d. D. Spr. II, p. 666, is of opinion, that the pret. eade, for the W. S code (which also occurs; f. i. Li. Lu, 1, 22; 4, 30; etc.), is worth a particular notice. It may, however, be permitted to suggest, that the change of the W. S. code into the N. A. cade is nothing but the change of o into a, which nearly all verbs of Rask's I. 1 in the N. A. have been subjected to.

[8]) The pl. sint (sindon) is, however, of frequent occurrence: gie sint ða tuiggo Li. J. 15, 5; bioðon 1 sint in cyninga husum Li. Mt. 11, 8; gie sint gelico ibm 24, 27; fulla sint mið deadra banum ibm: ðaðe upp sindon soccað Rit. p. 25, 3. — Sint looks rather Friesian.

[9]) As for the sens conveyed by bian, it is the same as in the common A. S. cf LATHAM, Hndbk of the Engl. Lang., 4 ed. p. 352

[1]) Here we must remark, that the regular verbs of the N. A. are

ic doam Li. Mr. 11, 33, and often; ic doom Li. J, 13, 7; ne dom ic Li. Mt. 20, 13; Rit. p. 59, 1, and often; ic geseam Li. J. 4, 19; ic gescom Li. Mr. 8, 24; ic nu gesium Li. J. 9, 25; ic sium Rit. p. 44; ic cuedon Li. Mt. 6, 25 [2]). But in most instances m is dropt, and the naked vowel, on its way to e hesitating between *a, o, u*, remains alone: ic halsa ðec Li. Mt. 26, 63; ic halgiga Li. J. 17, 19; ic milsa Li. Mr. 8, 2; ic iuih fulwa Li. Mt. 3, 11; ne doema ic Li. J. 12, 47 — are the only instances of *a* occurring in 1 pr. ind. sg. I am aware of; in general it is obscured into *o* or *u*, more seldom into *e*:

ic hrippo ðer ic ne seawu Li. Mt. 25, 26; ic fehto, iorne, mersigo Rit. p. 6, 3; ic cymo hine to wordianne Li. Mt. 2, 8; ic aedeawu Li. Lu. 12. 5; ic undoe Li. Mr. 14, 58 [3]).

In II sg. ind pres. *t* is nearly always dropt, and the verb terminates in *s*, *a* being sometimes obscured into *ae*, or softened into *e*, or *i*. The ð of III sg. and the pl. is generally softened down into *s*, whereby they terminate quite as II sg. [4]):

---

now and then, very irregular, in so far as the same verb does not constantly follow the same class of Rask's simple W. S. conjug., but, by means of inserting or dropping the derivative vowels, follows now the one scheme, now another.

[2]) Mr BOUTERWEK (p. CLV) finds in these examples only a "nunnation," proving a late redaction of the N. A. monuments. If so, m in the W. S. com and beom (GRIMM, D. Gr. I, 909, cf. p. 835), the Moes. Goth. im; the O. High. Germ bim. (Gr. p. 881), tuom (p. 885); the O. Saxon dôm (p. 894) and binm; the O. Norse em; — is. I suppose, also produced by nunnation. On the contrary, I think that a high antiquity may safely be vindicated to the N. A. forms in question. For this speaks also the preservation of a, not only in those positions where a following consonant may have contributed to its being preserved, but also, sometimes, where it stands quite naked: in 1 pres. ind., and in the subj., while in the W. S. it had long since — in 1 pr. ind. sg.; the one of the two pl. terminations, pres. subj. sg., etc. — run its whole course down to e. We shall in the following see, that this retaining of *a* can, perhaps, be ascribed to another cause.

[3]) That o or u here are more original than W. S. e, the W. S. forms hafu, or hafo, used in poetry, evidently prove. VERNON, A. S. Guide, p. 44.

[4]) Starting from the W. S. conjug., I have in the text considered

ðu faestas Li. Mt. 6, 17; lufas ðu mec Li. J. 21, 16; hu leornas ðu Li. Lu. 10, 26; ðu oferginas ibm 10, 35; ðu laeres, eftsceawes Li. Mt. 22, 16; seðe loses Li. Mt. 10, 39; seðe untynes 1 toslittes ibm 5, 19; seðe (mið) mec- ettaes Li. Mr. 14, 18; (hia) misbegaas hiora onsione Li. Mt. 6, 16; (hia) genimmaes ðec ibm 4, 6; ðer ðeafas ofdelfes 1 hrypes and forstealas

the II sg. in *st* as the more original form. — It is true that RAPP, Vergleichende Gramm. 1. p. 58, regards *sta* as the primit. terminat. of this person, but it is still more true that his opinion is contradicted. Is the s of *legis* etc. grown out from the t of the Sanskrit pron. tva (cf. BOPP, Vergleichende Gramm. p. 640) it is difficult to conceive that the *t* of II sg. in A. S. etc. is original. GRIMM, D. Gram. 1. p. 835, gives as the mark of II sg. *s* (Old-Norse, r), which is found troughout in all the most ancient dialects, while in the same dialects from the later portion of the middle-ages st has been substituted for *s*. I think we may be right in supposing this t to be nothing but the t of the pron. pers. thu, as the practice of affixing this pronoun (the true nature of the verbal terminations in the lapse of time having been forgotten) to the verbs is of very frequent use in all the Teuton. languages. It is already observed that, when this subjunction takes place, ð is changed into t. — Respecting the transition of the ð of III sg. pres. ind., and the plural, into s, it is no easy matter to produce full evidence. Is it identical with, the O. N. *s* of the same form, which at the time of the Scandin. colonisations in England, not yet had been changed into *r*, but by the Vikings was directly imported, and substituted for the ancient ð? For such a supposition speaks a remark of Rapp (l. c. p. 67), who says: der Scandier hat sehr abnorm statt des *t* der dritten Person das *r* (= s) aus der zweiten übertragen. — But it may be objected to it, that the O. N. conjug. possessed ð: that, consequently it is difficult to conceive why the Northmen should have slighted it in the A. S. Besides, the change is too vast to have been effected by a handful of foreigners. — There remains, then, only to suppose that ð has passed over into *s* (cf GRIMM, Gesch. d. D. Spr. 1. p. 353) in consequense of the same tendency that effected this change in the South-English, although many centuries later. We can, at least, not fancy that a Scandinavian influence was at work also there. — Here I cannot but think of some ingenious remarks of EDWARDS, concerning the preservation of the aspirated consonants in the German languages. I refer the reader to his Recherches sur les langues Celtiques, p. 6, 12, — putting for the further consideration of the same reader the question: were the ancient Britons more completely driven out of the North than the South of England?

ibm 6, 19). The forms in ð occur often. But ð was probably only an accommodation to the W. S. orthography, and in the N. A. verbs always pronounced s.

That for the apocopated W. S. pl. in -e, in N. A. *a, o, u*, sometimes occur, from what before is said of the interchange taking place between these vowels, need not be proved by special examples. — The subj. pres. ends in *a, o, e*, both in sg. and (the *n* being dropt) pl. This agrees closely with the O. Friesian.

ic neðdarf hafo, þ ic geonga and þ ilca gesea Li. Lu. 14, 18; ðeah se widewarda efuearisa Li. Mr. 3, 26; forlet hia l ða, þte hia geonga Li. Mr. 6, 36; þte hia ne losiga in woeg Li. Mt. 15, 32; and ic hia l ða haelo Li. Mt. 13, 15; gecyde him, þte hia ne aec ða cymo Li. Lu. 16, 28; (*o* is, in general, seldom met with); gearua, þte ic hriordlige Li. Lu. 17, 8; ic biddo þ ðu hine sende ibm 16, 27; þte — (he) hrinae ibm 16, 24; ne habbas þ hia ette Li. Mt. 15, 32.

We have, intentionally, until now deferred to treat of the use of *i* for *e* and *a*, which constitutes a remarkable feature of the N. A. conjug. It is particularly in the pres. ind. and subj. that this substitution takes place, but now and then also in pret. and the participles, as later will be shown ⁵): seðe gesiið Li. Mt. 6, 4; (geseað); ic ðe cueði Li. J. 21, 18; gesiistu Li. Mr. 13, 1; (he) ðe gesilið Li. J. 11, 22; (geseles); woenist Li. Lu. 18, 8; (woenes); haefis Li. Mt. 8, 9 (haefes), fliid Li. J. 10, 12, gefiið l gefiað Li. J. 15, 23; subj.: þte ic gesii Li. Mr. 10, 51, and often; geuuni Li. J. 21, 22; maegi Li. 21, 25.

All the here given forms are of frequent occurrence. — This *i* appears to have originated in different ways. The W. S. y in flyhð is in the N. A. fliið dissolved into *ii*. In gesii, geuuni etc. it may be the *i* of the O. Norse conjugation, although it is difficult to affirm it for quite certain.

Respecting the pret., we have already observed the N. A. practice of substituting *a* for W. S. *o* in I, 1 of Rask ⁶). There

---

⁵) The words within brackets give the more common forms.

⁶) Sometimes a stands even for the terminating e: waelda; Li. Mt. 14, 7; gehalgada Li. J. 17, 19; coda Li. Lu. 24, 12. — worhtae Rush. Mt. 25, 16. is scarcely worth mentioning.

3*

remains to show, that the 11 sg. indic. was -es rather than -est[7]): ðu geondsuaredes Li. Lu. 10, 28; ðeu gdeigeldes Li. Mt. 11, 25; ðu aedeavades Rit. p. 2. 1: ðu gesyngades Rit. p. 11. 14: gilesdes Rit. p. 29, 32: gibrohtes Rit. p. 31, 11: givdes Rit. p. 32, 18; gisaldes Rit. p. 47, 6; giefendes Rit p. 57.

Est occurs beside es. May it perhaps be considered as a W. S. import? — The *n* of the pl. indic. as well as subj. is not seldom thrown away, and (*o*) *u* softened into *e*:

ue saegnade Li. J. 8, 48; gie unwordade Li. J. 8, 49; hia gebreco Li. J. 19, 31; gie ne placgade. woepde Lu. 7, 32; gie gelefde Li. J. 5, 46; hia gefrugno Li. Mr. 11, 31; hia woere Li. Lu. 23, 32; gie ne wero Li. Lu. 16, 12; (hia) foerde Li. J. 6, 21 [8]).

About the imperat. there is very little to say. S stands usually for ð, and in the vowels there reigns the usual vacillation.

The infin. has dropt the *n*, and *a* is not seldom transformed into *ae* or *e*:

gibidda Rit. p. 11, 14; unrotsiga Rit. p. 12, 24; gimonigfaldiga Rit. p. 13, 29; toslita, toworpa, getimbra Li. Mt. 26, 61; eatta ibm 25, 35; losiga Li. Lu. 13, 3; lufia Li. J. 15, 19; bifoa Li. J. 21, 25; gesea Li. Mt. 11, 8; — maemae Li. Mt. 9, 15; woenae ibm 5, 17; gehorogae, gehydae Li. Mr. 14, 65; gebege Li. Lu. 9, 12; gestyrige ibm 9, 49; gewidlige Li. Mr. 7, 18; sende Li. Mr. 6, 7; gewyrce ibm 6, 5; losige Li. Mt. 10, 39.

What has been said above concerning the adjectives, finds its application also as to the participles; and there only remains to give examples of *i* used in them. They are rather few, and, for aught I am aware of, only found in Li. J.: gisaeh ðone ilca ambeh fylgendi 21, 20; ða ilco boee bifoa, ðaðe to auritteni sint 21, 25; þte ðio writt neri gifillid 19, 28, 30; uaes-sprec-

---

[7]) Which of the two is the more ancient, es or est? — The comparison with the M. Goth., O. High. Germ., O. Saxon, and O. Norse. shows that es is more common than est. It would consequently be rather precipitate to conclude that the N. A. es is the curtailed W. S. est.

[8]) The subj. ueri Li. J. 19, 28 etc. may here be mentioned as rather resembling the O. Norse uaeri.

cendi 12, 41. — Before leaving the verbs, the practice of suffixing the personal pronouns to verbal forms, the *n* of the pl. then being dropt and the *o*, generally, shortened into *e* or *i*, must be mentioned. The *o* of 1 pres. sg. etc. is thrown off, when the pron. sufixed begins with a vowel [9]).
willic Li. Mt. 15, 32; leornadege ibm 12, 3; wallige Li. Mr. 15. 12; onfengige Li. Mt. 16, 10; cadege Li. Mt. 11, 8; ne cudugie Li. Lu. 11. 49. More examples may be had nearly on every page of the Li. [1]).

The analysis of the N. A. dialect, as this presents itself in the Rit. and Li. Gospels, now being absolved, we shall procede to the examination of the other monuments said to belong to this dialect. — Of Caedmon's hymn to the creator, in the *not* W. S. redaction, I have before me two copies, the one printed by Conybeare [2]) from Wanley, the other given by Mr Thorpe [3]). from Smith's edition of King Alfred's Bede. The last has six readings differing from the corresponding ones of the first. Four of these [4]) deserve no particular attention, whereas it would

[9]) ðn, affixed, becomes tu: ondsuarestu Li. J. 18, 28.
[1]) This practice, I think, has not a little contributed to the dropping of n in the pl. of pres. subj. and the preter. Has it also produced the apocopated W. S. pl. indic. pres.?
[2]) Illustrations of A. S. Poetry, p. 6.
[3]) Thorpe's Caedmon p. XXII.
[4]) The readings at variance are:

Mr Thorpe	Conybeare
or astelidæ	ora stelidae
scop	scopa
aelda	elda
fold	foldu
halig	haleg
dryctin	drictin.

I am of opinion that elda is more N. A. than aelda, whereas halig is more N. A. than haleg. As for scopa (W. S. scapan, scop), I think that it is a very characteristic sign of a N. A. origin of the fragment in question. It is, indeed, particularly in Li., not uncommon to find a vowel in the same way affixed to the preterit of the strong verbs: and miððy (he) gecuome in Li. Mt 21, 23; seðe fif craefte onbo very interesting to get full evidence concerning the two remaining ones. The common text of Alfred's Bede having: firum foldan, Wanley reads: firum foldu, and Mr Thorpe: firum fold. Foldu agrees completely with the forms of the Durham glosses, while fold may be accounted for as: = foldu. folde with e dropt. Both readings, then, are equally legitimate, but not like interesting in our point of view. Is the fragment, as Wanley thinks, from the 8th century [5]), foldu, if the true reading, shows that the nouns, which in W. S. took -an in all cases, except the nomin. followed, already at that time, the same rules as in the Durham Glosses. The pl. in -ana proves however sufficiently, that, at a more remote period, these nouns must have followed the same scheme as the corresponding W. S. nouns. Foldu, then, met with in the 8th century, only pushes back the question respecting the dropping of -n in the nouns to a time anterior to that century; but shows, at the same time, that this dropping

---

fenge ibm 25, 16. — Mithinks that I have also found *ae* so affixed, and the vacillation among *a, ae, o, u* makes it credible, that also these may sometimes have stept into the place of *e*.

[5]) Conybeare (l. c.) is of opinion that it is the work of the 11th or 12th century. We cannot here enter into a discussion of the reasons pro and con., and confine ourselves to the following remarks:

1) the orthography of the fragment of Caedmon is, in all material points, the same as that of the Ruthwell Cross; there is consequently not the least doubt of the frag. being N. A.;

2) Scopa (see the preced. note) and foldu are N. A. peculiarities; so are: maceti W. S, (mihtig), uard (W. S. weard), barnum (W. S. bearnum), heben (W. S. heofon), aerist (W. S. aerest), and, finally, astelidae (W. S. onstealde) cf. smiridi Li. J. 9, 11, and gi-for ge-;

3) the *n* in the infin. hergan makes it probable, that the fragment is more ancient than the N. A. Gospel-Glosses and the Ruthwell Cross, but, as it stands quite isolated, too great stress is not to be laid on this fact;

4) the occurrence of the prepos. til, never found in W. S. M. S. S., except the last portion of the Saxon-Chron., is no proof of the speech in the district where the fragment was transcribed having been influenced by the Scandinavian tongue. Besides being twice found in the Li. (Mt. 26, 17, 31), til occurs in the O. Friesian, Grimm, D. Gr. II, p. 257. It will afterwards be shown, that Friesians probably partook of the colonisation of Northumbria.

of *n* was not the result of foreign influence, but of a tendency to that effect, pervading the N. A. dialect. — We cannot any longer dwell upon this fragment, and leave it, referring those who wish for further particularities to HALBERTSMA's elaborate analysis of it in the Introduc. to BOSWORTH's A. S. Diction., p. LVI.

The fragment known as the death-bed verses of Bede is from a M. S. at St. Gellen. KEMBLE [6]) thinks that it may, in its present shape, safely be referred to the year 737. — Of this I have also before me two printed copies [7]), but unfortunately not so agreeing with each other, that there could only be question of a few various readings. That given by CONYBEARE is nearly at every word differing from that printed by LATHAM, being, for aught I can see, tolerably good W. S., whereas the latter seems in many points approaching the N. A. forms. Thus uuirthit (Cony. wyrðeð), tharf (Con. ðearf), sie (Con. sy), hionongae (Con. heonan-gange), doemid (Con. demed), are undoubtedly pure N. A. [8]). As for the orthography, Latham's copy agrees closely with that of the inscription on the Ruthwell Cross, which forms the next topic of our inquiry [9]).

Not being able to enter upon a minutious analysis of the language of this inscription, we shall confine ourselves to showing forth its most remarkable features. — In the first place we remark, that there is not the least clue to find out its age. The

---

[6]) Procd. of the Philol. Soc. II, p. 124.

[7]) The one in CONYB. Illustrat. of A. S. Poetry, p. 8, the other in LATHAM's Hndbk of the Engl. Lang. (4 ed.) p. 139; where, if I am right, it is reprinted from KEMBLE'S paper in the XXVIII vol. of Archæologia. Want of access to this latter work prevents giving any particularities concerning the M. S. — Conyb. does not say, that he gives it from the St. Gallen M. S., but no more does he quote his source.

[8]) We refer the reader to the preceding analysis of the N. A., especially to what concerns the use of *i* for W. S. *e*.

[9]) Those, who wish to know the interesting history of this venerable monument are referred to the accounts given by KEMBLE, Archæologia, XXVIII p. 327; XXX, p. 31, and WILSON, Archæ. and Prehist. Annals of Scotl. p. 543. Also Dr SIMPSON, in his Address to the Society of Antiquaries of Scotl., 1861, p. 66, relates the principal facts relative to it. The text used is Kemble's, Arch. XXVIII, p. 357.

language, however, appears to be from about the time when the Li. and the Rit. were executed. It agrees with these in the grammat. forms and in some points of orthography, differing from them particularly in the frequent substitution of ae for e: darstae (cf. walda, halgada), geredae, gamaeldae. (these preter. plead perhaps for presuming walda and halgada not to be more slips of the pen, but then still current forms; supposed that ae was anything more than a peculiar manner of writing the slender e); hinae (Li. Rit. hine), hiae : fusae (not found in the other N. A. monuments; it might in Li. and Rit. have been written: fusa, fuso, fuse); aeðdilae. As points of agreement we observe: the *i* of rodi (W. S. rod, f.) hifunaes (hefon Li. Lu. 4, 25), ni (for ne), ti (to; til with the l dropped?) — gistiga, giwundaed (ge W. S.; gi Li. Rit.) and the last *i* in niðbaedi; the *n* being dropped in the infinitives: gistiga, haelda, and in the pl. preter. cwomu; (The last KEMBLE considers as only a carelessness, but, I think, not with full reason); the twice occurring dative galgu (an (= on) galgu, mid ga(l)gu). As such may, perhaps, also the *u* in pl. preter., instead of *o*, be regarded: alegdun, gistoddun. The occurrence of the dual-form ungket in the Ruthwell Runes is already pointed out [1]).

We now procede to try answering the question put long ago: is the Cotton Psalter North-Anglic? — We observe in it the following points of agreement with the undoubtedly N. A. monuments:

u in 1 pres. indic.: ne ondredu ic Ps. 3, 7; ic cliopin 4, 4; ic gebidu 5, 4; ic ondettu, singu, 3, 18; ic gefio 9, 16; ic gebreocu 17, 43;

a for *o* in preter. 1, 1: ic kneappade 3, 6; ic aldade 6, 8; ðu ge-steadulades 8, 4; haltadon 17, 46; du ge-lustfullades

---

[1]) It is remarkable enough, that traces of the dual of the pers. pronouns are found neither in the Li. nor in the Rit. I give the following passage, as one where dualforms might have been expected: Li. Mt. 20, 32: huaet wallað gie þ ic iuh gedoa — — þte usna ego sic untynde.

THORPE ibm: Hvaet wylle gyt þaet ic inc do? — — þaet uncre eagan syn geopenode.

29. 2; ge-cadmodade 34. 13; ðu neasades 16, 3; gereafadon 43, 11; ge-freades 43, 8;

a for *o* in the past part. 1, 1: gesweotulad 16, 15 ²);
oe for W. S. *é*: gedroefed 6, 8, 11; gemoeted 16, 3; gecoeled 38. 14; doem mec 42, 1;
— as (-es) in 11 pres. sg. ind.: ðu neosas 8. 5; ðu ineardas 5. 12; ðu geheres. 5, 4;
— es in II pret. ind.: ðu geherdes, gebreddes 4, 2; ðu saldes 4, 7 (see also above), but, as in the other N. A. M. S. S., also, -est.

As discrepancies we observe: the *n* never being dropped, neither in the infinitives, nor in pl. subj. pres., nor in the nouns of the simple order;

a or *o* never occurring in subj. pres.; ð never being softened down to *s; i* never, or very seldom, substituted for the W. S. *e*, and, upon the whole, showing a considerably more restricted range than in Li., Rit., and the fragments. — Which now claim the greater consideration, the discrepancies, or the conformities? I presume the former, for the following reasons. — We have seen that there exists a series of written monuments which undoubtedly are N. A., composed between the year 740 (or thereabout) and the end of the 10th century. We have further seen, that the dialect, due allowance made for the vacillating orthography, is, in all material points, the same in the fragments of Caedmon's hymn, the death-bed verses of Bede, and the runic inscription of the Ruthwell Cross, as in the Rituale Dunelmense, the Li. Gospels, and the last portion of the Rushworth gloss. Are WANLEY, and others, right in assigning the first of these documents, as well as the second, to the 8th cent., we have reason to suppose, that the N. A. already at that remote time had assumed some of its peculiar marks. — Can the inscription of the Ruthwell Cross be referred to a more remote age, as its runic character, and the pronomin. form ungket, only found there and nowhere else in all the Old-German documents [6]),

---

²) I turn the readers attention to the first a in aldade, haltadon = W. S. *ea*.

³) Ungket is by KEMBLE (l. c.) looked upon as an "incontrovertible proof of extreme antiquity."

tend to show; there are strong reasons for supposing the N. A., already hundreds of years prior to the interlineation of the Durham Glosses, having been on the way to that stage of development in which it there meets our eyes.

The age of the Cotton Psalter cannot be ascertained. The Latin text seems to be as old as the 8th century⁴), the interlineary gloss, consequently, can scarcely be older than the end of that, or the beginning of the following century, that is to say, not older than the N. A. fragment of Caedmon and the death-bed verses. Were it N. A., it ought, then, to exhibit the same peculiarities as the latter documents, but we have observed that the *n* after vowels is never dropped, and that the substitution of *i* for *e*, so prominent a feature in the orthography of the two fragments, the Ruthwell runes, and the Durham Glosses, is not used in the Psalter. The one as well as the other may with reason be considered as evidence against it being N. A. — As for the coincidences between the Psalter and the Glosses etc., the use of *oe* for W. S. *e* is, no doubt, the most remarkable. If, however, nothing more conspire with this *oe*, it cannot on its own account be considered as sufficiently proving a N. A. parentage⁵). The other points of agreement are scarcely of a more convincing kind. *U (o)* ⁶) in sg. pres. indic. is not exclusively N. A,, it is only the more ancient form, as a comparison with the Moeso-Goth., O. H. Germ., O. Saxon, sufficiently shows. We have already mentioned the W. S. hafu or hafo ⁷), which proves that in that dialect, as in others, o had in the lapse of time been superseded by e. The a ⁸) in the preter. and past. part., for W. S. *o*, may in the same way also be more ancient than this latter vowel. — Concerning II sg. pres. ind. in -as, and II sg. preter. indic. in -es, we remark that the dropping of *t* is not exclusively N. A. — If our premises are true, and we do give them as subject to doubt, the Cotton Psalter is

---

⁴) KEMBLE, Philol. Proced. (l. c.).

⁵) Cf. p. 20 (in the note).

⁶) The Psalter's want of m in this form seems also worth attention, as contributing to prove it not N. A.

⁷) p. 33, note.

⁸) This a will be further spoken of in the following.

not North-Anglic. What it is, we leave to the decision of others. GARNETT [8]) thinks that it originated somewhere in Mercia, and this opinion may be as right as any other which might be substituted for it. We may, perhaps, even venture to say that it was in the North of Mercia, as its language seems affine to the N. A. — We remind here of Bede stating Mercia to have been peopled by Angles.

The preceding analysis of the North-Anglic dialect has shown, that, already towards the end of the 10th century, it had reached a stage of development which in many respects left far behind it the South-Saxon, even in that shape which this attained in the last portion of the Saxon Chronicle, the Legend of St. Katherine from Alexandria, and even Layamon's Brut. — Whence this broadly marked difference of development? Can it have been brought about "alanerly" by the external influences, which worked upon the dialects of the South and the North in quite dissimilar ways? — If it is so, well, then all the peculiarities which distinguish the North-Anglic, as opposed to the common literary dialect of Saxon England, must, one and all, be referrible to the O. Norse; for we know no other language at work upon the N. A. dialect prior to the Norman conquest, as the Celtic is here not taken into account. Well let us see: perhaps will the dialect itself not turn "deaf as Ailsa Craig" to our patriotic [9]) wooings, as did the local names.

KEMBLE says [1]) that the Scandinavian mark of the infin., att, occurs in the Li. Gloss. This is considered an uncontrovertible proof of Scandin. influence. We will in the following inquire into the truth of the latter assertion; here we remark that att, or (as it probably would have been in the orthography of the Li.) at, is *not* found · in this gloss, neither in Mr BOUTERWEK's edition, nor in the Gospel of St. Matth. published

---

[8]) Philol. Essays p. 183.
[9]) For the sake of such foreigners as may happen to be my readers, I beg leave to mention, that I boast a descent from the England-conquering Danes, being a thorough-bred Sconian from time immemorial.
[1]) Phil. Proceedings. II, p. 124.

by Mr STEVENSON [2]). Li. Mr. 14, 1, occurs the word et: uut et aefter twaem dogrum, which might be regarded as the Scand. conjunct. att, and, indeed, is identical with it. But in the following part of our researches it will be demonstrated to full evidence, that this at is no more imported to England from Scandinavia than the Latin ut is the from Greece imported ὅτι. — It is true, that the practice of throwing off the terminating *n*, when preceded by a vowel, is a practice pervading the Northern languages, and constituting one of their most characteristic properties [3]). But this peculiarity is also met with in the O. Friesian [4]). — The change of *a* into *u*, often taking place in the N. A. nouns of the Simple Order after the dropping of n, may be of Scandinavian extraction; as we see this vowel prevail in the O. Norse fem. nouns of the Simple Order [5]); and, as we find in the language of the Glosses a great confusion of gender, we may easily imagine how *u* can be found also in nouns of the masc. or neut. gender, as well as in those of the fem. Hither the custom of retaining *u* in all cases of Rask's III, 2, 3, may be, can also be referred.

Further, I think, the practice of affixing the masc. genit. termination to fem. nouns, both of the Simple and Complex Order, may safely be ascribed to Northern influence. An allusion

---

[2]) bye, by Garnett, Phil. Ess. p. 182, considered as one of the articles of North. import, is spoken of p. 8, (note). — I remark here, that bu, expressing the same meaning as in O. Norse, is found in the Mid. H. Germ.; see ZIEMANN, Mittelhochdeutsches Wörterbuch, sub voc. bu.

[3]) cf. Grimm, D. Gr. I, p. 305.

[4]) l. c. p. 275. — It may here be observed that Orm's (mark the dropt W!) Paraphrase of the Gospels, which in other respects exhibits the effects of Scand. influence (cf. WHITE's ed. I, p. LXXVII), and most likely originated in East-Anglia (ibm p. LXXV), where we know many Danes to have settled, never drops the *n* of the infin., and has quite as much left of the *n* of the Simple Order as any South-English M. S. of the same period.

[5]) It must however not be overlooked, that this obscuration, on the *n* being dropt, very well may have taken place in the naked vowel without any external influence.

to the *s* in the gen. of Moeso-Gothic fem. nouns is in every respect here out of place, as this *s* has disappeared from the O. High Germ. and O. Saxon, not to mention the O. Friesian [6]). Perhaps might the occurrence of such forms as: eorðes, maehtes, naehtes, sunes, woruldes in the N. A. be used as collateral evidence for proving that the *r* of the O. Norse jardar, maktar, naetr (nattar), sonar, woruldar, had not yet made its appearance when the Danish wikings settled in England. The change of gender, following the change of termination, is then easily accounted for: as the Angles for centuries had been accustomed to look upon all nouns with gen. in -es as masc. or neut., the stuck to the old practice, and made also the fem., when taking the masc. termination, masc. or neut.

The *i* [7]) of the dat. sg. in biscopi, caseri etc. is probably the *i* of the dat. of the O. Norse Complex Order; in the same way as the final *i* of oðri, awritteni etc. may be the *i* of the O. Norse pl. termination -ir, and *i* in fylgendi the *i* of the nom. sg. masc. of the adjectives, in the defin. declension, and the present participle, here retained in the acc., its proper use having been forgotten.

Respecting the remains of a pl. termination in-r, given p. 28. it is only safe to assert that, at this time, the pl. *s*, both in the O. Norse and the O. Friesian, had effected its transition into *r*.

The *a* in the N. A. preter. and past. part. is as much O. Friesian as O. Norse [8]). Besides, it appears very reasonable to suppose that the *o* in the preter. and past part. of the W. S. 1, 1 is nothing but an obscuration of an original a.

The *i* in the verbs (p. 35) seems to be of Northern extraction. But it may be observed, that, if the age assigned to the N. A. fragments is the true one, it becomes more than questionable, if this supposition keeps good. I think, however, that the range of *i* in the verbal forms of the dialect of North-England and Scotland, during the 14th and 15th centuries, rather

---

[6]) Cf. GRIMM, D. Gr. I, p. 616 etc.
[7]) Respecting the use of *i* for *e* in the O. Friesian cf. l. c. p. 270.
[8]) Cf. GRIMM, D. Gr. I. p. 911.

tends to show that it was a foreigner, who bye-and-bye, got domesticated.

The pl. pres. ind. of wosa, aron, in all persons, resembles undoubtedly the O. Norse erum, and the dropping of *w* before the following *e*, and the *r*, unquestionably grown out of an original *s*, appear rather somewhat Scandin. Its very common occurrence in the Glosses is, however, of a nature to make us a little doubtful about its true origin.

The last peculiarity of the N. A. that coincides with the practice of the Old-Norse is the dropping of *w* before *u, o, y* [9]); instances are given p. 22; but at the same time there has been shown, that *w* is often put before vowels without the least reason. Perhaps it is the same thing with the one as the other, and both may be nothing but carelessness. [1]).

— — —

If we now draw the consequences of what hitherto has been developed, they are: that in the North-Anglic dialect very little [2]), and that little, to boot, very questionable, bears the mark of having been imported from Scandinavia; while, on the other hand, we find, that the N. A. nearly in every point agrees with the O. Friesian. It is true the monuments we possess of this latter language are considerably yonger than the N. A. Glosses and poetical fragments; and the objection might be made that a comparison between those monuments and the Friesian of the Asega-book is not authorised, there being too long an interval of time between them. Against this objection I set the opinion of Grimm, who [3]), respecting the Friesian, says, that there is strong reason for believing that in the 9th century it was the

---

[9]) Cf Grimm, Gesch. d. Deut. Spr. I, p. 297.

[1]) The substitution of the pl. of the dem. pron. for the true pl. of the person. pron., no doubt a Scand. practice, will be examined in the following part.

[2]) The single words which may have been introduced from these quarters are, of course, not here taken into account.

[3]) Gesch. d. D. Spr. II. p. 668. — p. 680, he remarks that masc. nouns of the Complex Order often take the gen. in -ena of the Simple Order; a point of agreement with the N. A. which is well worth noticing.

same as some centuries later: whereby the authorisation to make such a comparison is given. — The question which then rises: were there any Friesians in England, cannot here be treated at large; we must confine ourselves to a few remarks. — Did the name Friesians, as Zeuss [4]) conjectures, mean: Wagenden, Muthigen, or, as Grimm [5]) seems inclined to think: Free, it is clear, that this name, as that of the Franks, was not the name a single tribe, but of a confederation of kindred tribes, among of whom each tribe at the same time had its own specific denomination [6]). In this manner, the Angles may pretty well have been Friesians in the wider sense of this word. Perhaps did they lose this name after their having settled in England, when they no longer belonged to the Friesian confederation, retaining only their specific denomination. This may be the cause why Bede, himself an Angle, does not speak about their being Friesians. To an external observator these facts, however, would have presented themselves somewhat differently. Such an author, knowing the generic name of Friesians, and knowing that migrations to Britain had taken place among them, but ignorant of the specific names of the tribes, that lurked under the common appellation, would naturally have said that Friesians had emigrated to England. Should the author have happened to know the specific name of one of the tribes partaking of the emigration, but not those of the others, he might have put the generic name together with the specific one, and in this way brought about a confusion of both. — Now Procop [7]) tells us that Angles and Friesians dwelled in Britain. Is it wrong to suppose a confusion lurking in this statement, and to suppose that Angles and Friesians here are synonymes?

But we must stop pursuing this course of conjectures, and take up another question presenting itself all along with the preceding supposition.

[4]) Die Deutschen u. die Nachbar Stämme p. 136 (note).
[5]) l. c. p. 670.
[6]) It may be that the common name in after years was more exclusively applied to a single tribe.
[7]) De bello Gothico lib. IV, 20.

It has been shown, that the N. A. dialect retained a not inconsiderable number of forms more ancient than the corresponding W. S.: the *m* of 1 pres. sg. is very ancient, and that a, which once preceded it, is not yet throughout obscured into *o*, or this *o* softened into *e*, speaks for a retaining of the consonant-termination until a relatively late period. The same observation keeps good respecting the a of the pret. and the participles. On the other hand, we have observed a great confusion taking place as well in the nouns of the Simple Order, whose *e* appears rapidly advancing towards final dropping, as in point of gender. As for the latter, we have alluded at least to one source of this confusion. — As for the former, the immediate cause of it, or the dropping of *n*, has been shown to have taken place to a much wider extent in the N. A. than in the Old-Norse, which a comparison with this latter language will not fail to evince. Besides, allusion has been made to the remarkable fact of the terminating *n* having been preserved in East-Anglian monuments, which, in other respects, exhibit very marked signs of Scandinavian influence. — The final conclusion, as I hope pretty well borne out by all the preceding researches, is then this: the North-Anglic dialect stood long before any Scandinavian settlements ever were etablished in Northumbria in the same contrast with the West-Saxon as the Old-Friesian with the Old-Saxon. But it was stunted in its free development, on the one side, by the literary W. S. (we remind of our glosses having been written in the 10th century). to the influence of which the forms in *n*, now and then occurring in the glosses, and the modes of spelling not seldom approaching to the W. S. practice may probably be ascribed; while, on the other side, the Old-Norse may have modified the N. A. in more than one respect, although its influence, as has been shown, cannot, at least in what concerns the grammatical forms, be exactly appreciated. — Here we discontinue surveying the Old-North-Anglic. — A giants-bound — over a space of time not less than four hundred years — and we are face to face with that descendant of the Old-North-Anglic which we shall call

The Scoto-English Dialect.

The language spoken at the court of Malcolm Ceanmor was, no doubt, that branch of the Celtic tongue which goes under the name of Gaëlic. But it is no more subject to doubt, that that anglicizing tendency which, aided by the pressure of circumstances and the unhappy social state of England, succeeded in germanizing the Scotch Lowlands, under him took its beginning, although he did not himself keep the first place among the anglicizing kings of Scotland [8]). When and how the language of the "Southrons" became the language of the Scotch court, no one is able to say. It is also far from being certain, that, when the Gaëlic was banished, the Saxon, or N. A., immediately obtained the vacant office. We must remember that the new-comers were as often Normans as Saxons. and that the former by far had the greater credit, being the very flower of European chivalry. To assert that the Norman-French immediately succeeded the Gaëlic, is not safe against objections, but is quite as credible as the opinion, that the Saxon was immediately substituted for the mentioned language [9]). It is known that, at the coronation of Alexander III, the oaths were taken by the king and his subjects first in Latin, afterwards in Norman French, and that political transactions, when not carried on in the former, were made in Norman-French. We do, however, nowise maintain that Saxon was not spoken in Scotland; only that its use was restricted to the lower classes, while the Norman-French was the language of the higher. This is, upon the whole, mere supposition; but a supposition backed by many reasons.

---

[8]) Cf. INNES, Scotl. in the M. A. ch. III.

[9]) — "we learn from a curious passage in the inedited Latin Chronicle attributed to Walter of Coventry, that as early as the reign of William the Lion (not still earlier?) the Scotish court had adopted the manners, dress, and even the language of France." Sir FRED. MADDEN, Syr Gawane, p. 337. TYTLER, Hist. of Scotl. II, p. 248, says: "the Norman-French — seems never, as in England, to have usurped the place of the ancient national dialect of the Scoto-Saxon". — Pray, what does Mr. T. mean by Scoto-Saxon as the ancient national dialect of Scotland? How has he found out that the native tongue of Malcolm Ceanmor was not the Gaëlic?

The earliest traces of Saxon language in Scotland, besides the Ruthwell Cross, are from the reign of William the Lion, in whose charters we meet with a few Saxon words [1]). There is further to be found an indenture of lease from the first years of the 14th century, the Latin text of which is interlined with phrases of the vernacular tongue [2]). But these two documents are of little avail to the student of the Scoto-English dialect as containing only a few unconnected words, and were they the only remains of it, we should be entitled to say nothing more than that in the middle-ages a Teutonic language was spoken in the Scotch Lowlands, but we should never be able to make out its peculiarities. Fortunately, the taste for romantical compositions was the same in Scotland, and the North of England, as in other parts of Europe, and in the romances penned in the former districts we have the earliest mediaeval monuments of some importance to our dialect. Beside these romances, chiefly treating the Table-Round, we find a paraphrase of the Psalter and some rhymed homilies, the one as well as the others, no doubt, among the most ancient monuments of our dialect, and, as more particularly calculated for the lower people, very remarkable for purity of language. while in the romances we meet with a speech strongly mixed up with French. That this should be the case, is sufficiently clear, partly. from what we already know of the Norman-French settlements in the north of England and the Scottish Lowlands, partly, from the necessity, in which every person longing for learning found himself, of studying in the university of Paris, as Scotland wanted every means of literary improvement until a relatively late period. We must also keep in mind, that between the courts of Scotland and France there existed, during the whole of the middle-ages, friendly relations and a frequent intercourse, and that, during the wars between France and England, strong bodies of Scotch soldiers were always engaged in French service, while, now and then, France also sent auxiliaries to Scotland. That the Scoto-English dialect was strongly influenced by the French is, under such circumstances,

---

[1]) INNES, Scotl. in the M. A. p. 254.

[2]) Printed by Mr Innes. The Brus, p. XVII; and Scotl. in the M. A. p. 334.

not to be wondered at. It was also worked upon by the dialects of South-England, while, at the same time, it appears in some respects to have contributed to the formation of the modern English tongue. In the following we shall try to point out the effects of this mutual interchange; here we only remind of the fact, that, during the intervals of the nearly continual wars between England and Scotland, many Scottish students repaired to the English universities, and a lively commercial intercourse found place between the subjects of the two crowns.

It has been remarked, that there exists in northern literature a complete vacuum of some four hundred years, a space of time entirely employed in intestine broils and rich in alterations in the social state of Britain. A sceptic might ask: is the dialect of North-England and the Scotch Lowlands the true descendant of the dialect of the Lindisfarne Gospels, etc.? Are any criteria of it being so to be found? We shall make an essay to answer the latter question, and, at the same time, to lay down the principles to be followed in judging of a M. S. belonging either to the Scoto-English, or to one of the South-English dialects. If what proves a M. S. to be Scoto-English, at the same time demonstrates its derivation from the practice of the Old North-Anglic, the former question is also answered, and the Scoto-English clearly shows itself as the descendant of the Old North-Anglic. It is true, that the one as well as the other ought, strictly speaking, first to come forth as the final results of the subsequent researches; but it is necessary, already here, partly to anticipate these final results in order to get a Scoto-English standard, with which we can contrast the M. S. S., and then decide what is true Scoto-English, and what is to be considered as properly belonging to the southern dialects and only adventitious in the former. — As the most prominent features of the S. E. we point out:

1) the *n* has disappeared from the nouns as well as from the infin., the preter. pl. and the pres. indic. and subj. pl.; traces of it being very rare and seldom met with; while in the southern dialects it is of very regular occurrence in all the forms alluded to;

2) the *th* of the verbs is everywhere softened into *s*, while

it is retained in the South-English. When *th* occurs in writings known to be Scotch, it may fairly be considered as an effect of Southern influence;

3) for the plur. of III pron. pers. they is regularly used;

4) the *i* has much encroached upon the territory of *e*, particularly in the pret. and past part., which, indeed, in the S. E. have become formally identical.

A comparison with the N. A. shows sufficiently: that 1 and 2 were two of its most characteristic peculiarities, as contrasted with the literary W. S.; that the demonstr. pron. was on the way to supersede the true pron. person.; and that *i* had a good deal of inclination for the places *e* possessed by ancient right. — It were an easy matter to multiply the evidence produced, and point out more characteristics of the S. E. But the marks given above are sufficient to set forth the diversity existing between this dialect and the Southern ones, and to prove its descent from the Old N. A.

As for the range of the S. E., it was the same as that of the O. N. A., due allowance made for the extension of the Teutonic territory of Scotland and the encroachments of the South-English dialect upon Northumbria, where the S. E. ceased to exist as literary tongue towards the end of the 15th century [2]). — We must still add some words concerning the foreign influences at work upon the North-Anglic. GARNETT observes [3]): "that the admixture of the Northmen in the population of Northumbria had not produced its full effect upon the language in the 10th century," whereas "in the 14th century the traces of this influence

---

[2]) The change seems to have been brought about by degrees, as afterwards in Scotland. Among the publications of the Surtees Society we find a volume entited: Wills and Inventories etc. (1835), where a few deeds in English (the greatest number being Latin) are met with, the language of which very much resembles the South-English. Such are LII, from York, and LV, from New-Castle. The language of the Towneley Mysteries, although in many points pure S. E., has a strong sprinkling of Southern. — GARNETT, Ph. Ess. p. 191, says the same of the York Mysteries, of which I have only had opportunity to see a short fragment, printed by him, l. c. p. 192.

[3]) Philol. Essays, p. 188.

become much stronger." These traces chiefly consist in words not found in the monuments of Saxon England, but appearing in the northern M. S. S. of the period we are now speaking of. It belongs therefore to etymological lexicography to trace their origin to the different sources, and show forth their quality of aliens. Although, then, it does not appertain to the plan of the present dissertation to enter upon researches of this kind, we will here make a step from the way traced before us, in order to give some observations respecting the three words: ger (gar), at (conjunct.), and at (preposit.), as these words are regarded as being, without any doubt, Scandinavian settlers to the North of the Humber, while their use in the Scoto-English constitutes one of the characteristic marks of this dialect [4]).

Verbs of the same root from which ger derives are to be found in the A. S., but ger itself is nowhere met with. Therefore, as it cannot well be supposed to be the A. S. gearcian, or gearwian, in an apocopated form, because this verb is never in A. S. used in the same way as ger in the S. E., it is very credible that ger is the O. Norse géra introduced into Northumbria, which has first had its terminating *a* softened into *e*, and then totally dropt, according to the prevailing practice. For this speaks, that gera was in the latter language used in the same manner as in the S. E., where it not only is a surrogate for the do of modern English, but also frequently occurs in the meaning of to cause [5]).

---

[4]) Respecting the words which, in all probability, were introduced into England by the Northmen, it cannot be doubted that tolerably long lists of them might be compiled: but it must be observed, that the compiler ought to be very circumspect, and bestow a good deal of care on his work, in order not to fall into the same errors as Mr WORSAAE, who, in a list consisting of 100 words, intended to show, "that the Scandinavian tongue must posses no mean degree of durability," introduces more than fifty which quite as well may be considered as pure A S. — W. l. c. p. 84.

[5]) To give examples of the use of ger in the S. E. is foreign to our purpose. Those who wish to know how it was used in the same way in the O. Norse and the modern Islandic are referred to: EGILSON, Lexicon Poëticum Antiquae Linguae Septentrionalis, s. voc. gera; and RYDQUIST, Svenska Språkets Lagar, 1. p. 496.

GRIMM [6]) seems inclined to derive the preposition at from the same source as the conjunction, and give both a common origin in the neutr. of the M. Gothic person. pronoun is; although it might appear somewhat singular that the derivate has the original vowel, while a in is has passed into i. Perhaps, the facts we are going to give will throw some light upon the formation of this conjunct., and make it probable, that it can have originated in another way, being the neuter of the demonstrative pron. se, seo, þaet. It is true, that the dropping of the beginning þ is not a fact of common occurrence, but the O. Norse enn, Sw. än, cannot well be regarded but as identical with the O. Sax. than and the A. S. þonne, which in the former tongue have dropped their þ. We further observe that at [7]) in the S. E. is not only a conjunction, in form and application identical with the Scand. at, but also very frequently fallen in with as a relat. pron. Now it sounds rather incredible that the latter practice should have grown out of the former, a pronoun originated in a particle, which indeed would have been the inverse of everything known concerning the formation of particles. It is therefore probable, that the conj. at, in the S. E., is of tolerably recent formation, homemade, and nowise imported. Were, however, the þ dropt only in the neut., there might still be some objections made to it having originated in England, and the use of at as a relat. pron. might be explained as having arisen from a confusion caused by the introduction of the Scandin. at. It might be fancied, that, as at was used for the A. S. conjunct. þaet (which in Northumbria, for any thing I know, might very well have changed its ae into a), it was, by confusion, also put for the relat. þaet. But the following examples, collected from the Northumbrian Psalter, show that þ was dropt before other words than the neut. þaet, consequently that we

---

[6]) D. Gr. II, p. 164.

[7]) For examples of the use of at as conjunct. see BOUCHER, Glossary of Archaic and Provincial Words, and JAMIESON, Scottish Dictionary, sub. v. at. Of its use as rel. pron. instances will be given in the following.

have a right of assigning the formation of at to the same quarters [8]):

>þai kalled to God, and he herd am;
>In beme of kloude he spake to þam. Ps. 98, v. 7.
>Laverd oure God, þou herd am swa
>Neghsom was tou unto þa. ibm v. 8.
>And he led am with silver and golde. Ps. 104, v. 37.
>Fained es Egipt in forthcome of am. ibm v. 38.
>And with brede of heven he filled am þenne. ibm. v. 40.

Many other instances might be quoted from the same source.

The origin of the preposition at we shall not meddle with; confining ourselves to the remark, that, under the form of aet, it is of frequent occurrence in the A. S.; and that, the infin. being a true noun, it might be used for its determination as well as any other preposition. There is however a consideration that makes me rather inclined to stoop to the common opinion of it being, as far as used as a mark of the infin., introduced by the Northmen. It is wanting in the Scotch proper; at least have I not been able to find it used in this way, neither in the Scotch writings I have had the opportunity of perusing, nor im JAMIESON's Scottish. Dict., while sometimes, although upon the whole not often, it is fallen in with in works penned to the south of the Tweed.[9])

Respecting the influence of the Gaëlic, it has scarcely gone so far as to cause any changes in the grammatical forms; but I am of opinion that, in other respects, it has contributed more

---

[8]) Is the O. N. A., as I have tried to prove, nothing but Friesian, the practice to drop the *th* of that etc. occurring in the latter language (see RASK, Frisische Sprachlehre §, 117) at least does not contradict my supposition.

[9]) For examples see BOUCHER's already cit. Gl. — In the Townely Mysteries it occurs twice, p. 189, in both instances joined with do. Is the ado of the actual English = at do of the Tow. M.? I am rather inclined to think it is, the interchange between the dialects of the North and the South having apparently taken place to an extent sufficient to acount for its being received into the latter.

to the diversity of the S. E. stock of words from that of South-English than the linguistic importations of the Northmen [1]).

We shall now give a few critical remarks concerning some of the works from which we have to gather information; confining them to those only which appear of a more dubious S. E. origin. — In the first decennium of this century, WALTER SCOTT discovered, in the Advocates' Library at Edinb., an ancient M. S., which he published under the name of Sir Tristrem, endeavouring at the same time, in the introduction prefixed to this romance, to prove that its authorship most likely must be ascribed to Thomas of Ercildoun, alias the Rhymer, so celebrated in Scotch popular tales. His opinion of Sir Tristrem being Scotch did not want partisans. CHALMERS, for one, in his edition of the Works of Sir DAVID LINDSAY [2]), declared that in Sir Tristrem we "have specimens of the language of Lothian at the time of Alexander III. "This was the opinion of CHALMERS, who, in his quality of author of Caledonia and editor of Old-Scottish works, ought to have been able to distinguish Scotch from English. The first who, from a literary-historic point of view, contradicted this opinion, if I am not mistaken, was PRICE [3]). His objections were afterwards followed up, from a more linguistical point of view, by the editors of the last (1840) edition of

---

[1]) I have picked up some hundreds of Gaëlic words only in the vol. 1 of JAMIES. Diction. — CHALMERS, Caledonia, vol. I, p. 446, shows that a good many terms of the (Old?) Scotch Laws are of Gaëlic origin. — TYTLER, l. c. p. 181, tells us that, in the latter half of the 12th century, great numbers of Flemings settled in Scotland. But to appreciate what influence these newcomers had on the formation of the S. E. is quite impossible, their speech, as a Low-German dialect, not being sufficiently distinct from the former dialect. There are, however, not a few words to be found in JAM. Dict. which closely agree with the Flemish, and, when they have relation to trade and manufactures, are not unlikely to have been introduced by these people.

[2]) I. p. 119. — As a specimen of Chalmers' manner of proceeding in philology the following may serve: Thir —" It is from the A. S. hiere (?!?!) illius (!!) with th prefixed, as it has been to several of the pronouns" (?!). Glossary to the W. of Sir D. L. s. voc. Thir.

[3]) In vol. II, appendix, of his edition of WARTON'S History of English Poetry.

Warton. Sir Fred. MADDEN even goes so far as to say: "the person, who made the English poem from the French — — I should think, might even have been a Londoner for anything the language says to the contrary [4]);" while GARNETT endeavours to show that Sir Tristrem, originally penned in Northumbria, from having been transcribed in a southern district, got its present shape only in the 14th century. This conjecture seems to me to come near the probability. In the language there is much that reminds of the S. E., but still more such as belongs to the South-English. Taking the first stanza of Fytte I, we find: thair for her, Tomas telles (South-E.—eth), and twice ware (usually in South-E.—en); all three S. E. peculiarities. But on the other hand we fall in with: who (S. E. wha, or quha); this aventours; of which particularly the pl. this is a sure mark of a South-English dialect. In other stanzas those "Southrons" occur in yet greater numbers.

The remarks made on the subject of Sir Tristrem keep good in respect to the old romances published by MADDEN under the name of Syr Gawayne [5]), although they do not alike apply to all of them. Thus, Syr Gawayne and the grene Knyzt is far less S. E. than: the awntyrs of Arthure at the Terne Wathelynne, and The knightly Tale of Golagros and Gawane. But, upon the whole, each of these three romances is far more true Scotch than Sir Tristrem, though, as far as known, none of them is written to the north of the Tweed. The reason of this is very simple, and has already been alluded to. The language of Northumbria was quite the same as that of the Scottish Lowlands; and had the former, as it indeed was during the latter half of

---

[4]) WARTON'S Hist. (1840) p. 109 — He also remarks (p. 111) that the constructions with genitives of personal pron., out of use in the English middle-age M. S. S. of a more recent date, speak for the relatively high age of Sir Tristrem. Such are: our on, one of us; whether our, whether of us; her aither, either of them; her bother, of them both; her non, none of them. — It may be, that these constructions speak for the antiquity of Sir Tristrem; but her (= heora) does not precisely plead its Northumbrian origin, as will soon be shown.

[5]) Respecting the M. S. S. of the mentioned romances, the reader is referred to Sir F. MADDEN'S introduction and remarks.

the 10th, and the first forty years of the 11th century, been kept in political union with Scotland, there cannot be the least doubt that its literary dialect would have continued the same as the Scotch, due allowance made for the influence the Gaëlic could have had on this more than on the speech of Northumbria.

This unity of dialect is clearly evinced by the Northumbrian versified paraphrase of the Psalter, and a very curious collection of rhymed homilies, published by Mr. SMALL [6]). To judge from the language in them, both appear to be from about the same time, probably the midst of the 14th century, and to have originated in the same quarters, in all probability somewhere in Northumbria. I know, however, nothing for certain, neither respecting their age, nor the precise locality where they were penned. Their language is pure. S. E.

It was originally our intention to give a somewhat complete account of the S. E. vowels and consonants, comparing them throughout with the corresponding South-English. But, it being obvious to us that this would too much surpass the limited number of sheets allotted to the whole of the present treatise, we drop this purpose, confining ourselves to a few remarks. Some others will incidentally be given in the following.

Mr. INNES [7]). on the stress of the interlineary indenture of lease already mentioned, says that "there cannot be a more pure English speech," the glosses being "without the redundancy of consonants, the gutturals, and many of the peculiarities, which,

---

[6]) During my stay at Edinburgh last summer, the editor of these homilies, then in course of being printed, had the kindness to permit my perusing the proof-sheets, and promised to send me a copy, as soon as any were ready. No one, however, having reached me, I regret much not being able to avail myself of these curious specimens of the dialect of Northumbria, by the editor pretended to be from the end of the 13th century (?), and being particularly remarkable for the great purity of their language, Norman-French words being altogether wanting, and the text exhibiting a pure A. S., stript of the terminations.

[7]) The Brus, pref. p. XVI.

in later times, gave an effect of coarseness to the language of Scotland in southern ears." Is what Mr Innes has given [6]), the whole of the interlineation, no conclusion can be less authorised than that quoted just now. It would, indeed, only be a matter of compiling to show that every one of the words occurring in the indenture is found, spelled quite in the same way, in the writings from the following century, and, as for the gutturals, I have run through the list more than once without being able to detect a single word where such might have been expected. His remarks, however, although not keeping good for the special case of the indenture, may perhaps, notwithstanding this, be quite true, and they therefore lead us to the question: was the guttural character of the S. E. an inheritance from the ancient Teutonic dialects, or was it produced by the intermixture of Gaëlic (whose guttural character appears to be of a very ancient date)? At first we observe that, in the decision of this question, all comparison with the English of the present day, and subsequent conclusions from its not guttural nature, must be excluded, it being tolerably certain, that its present want of gutturals is of later date, and produced along with the production of the originally simple vowel-sounds into diphthongs. This a comparison with the cognate dialects sufficiently shows. — We must, then, recur to the A. S., and more particularly to the N. A. — We observe here, that verbs, in the inf. having *c*, in the preter. took an *h*, and that nouns, in the nom. sg. terminating in *h*, in the oblique cases resume their gutturals. We may therefore with reason infer that the A. S. *h* in reality rather resembled the *ch* of the Old-Scotch. This is confirmed by the circumstance of the guttural sometimes being found instead of the spirans *h* in the nom. of nouns, and *ch* for *h* in preterits, etc. Some instances from the Li., as more particularly available to our purpose, may suffice: suachuelc Mt. 20, 26; lecht Mr. 13, 24; aðongh Lu. 8, 46; maeghte Mr. 8, 39; getrachtad J. 1, 41; bochton J. 4, 8; ðaech J. 4, 2; cf. also the forms of the N. A. pers. pronouns given p. 29. From these instances, and many others easily to be collected, I think it sufficiently clear that

---

[6]) In the above quoted works.

the Scottish forms: nocht, nicht, knicht, thoucht etc. are in reality quite equivalent to the A. S. miht, niht etc., the only change being the substitution of *ch* for *h* in the orthography, this *ch* having indeed always been the true pronunciation of the simple A. S. *h*. — I will, however, not deny that the Gaëlic may have had a certain influence on the retaining of the gutturals in Scotch, long after their having been done away in the pronunciation of the South-English.

Respecting the beginning *qu* of quhat, quha etc. it is difficult to produce full evidence. It can scarcely be considered as the original, interrog., *c*, being found not only in the interrog. and relat. pron., but also in most nouns which in the South-English are written with *wh*. No more can it be proved from the Old N. A. M. S. S. that *cw* already there was occasionally put instead of *wh* [9]). The Gaëlic, which retains the ancient interrog. *c* [1]), conjoint with the sharp guttural pronunciation of the A. S. *h*, may probably have brought about the change, which, doubtless, was more a matter of orthography than of pronunciation.

The retaining of *l* before a following *c (k)*, where the South-English, already in the 14th century, dropt the *l*, and changed *c* into *ch*, must also be mentioned as a characteristic mark of our dialect. Thus, this has: ilka, swylk, quhilk, etc., while the South-English forms are: ich (each), such, which, etc. The latter forms, fallen in with in the S. E. writings, are sure signs of an anglicizing author, and this the more so, because the forms with *l* are still used in the Braid-Scotch.

Respecting the vowels we observe that the S. E. much more closely sticks to the A. S. forms than the South-English. Thus, there is in the former a great predilection for the preservation af *a*, quite as was the case with the Old North-Anglic, while in the latter this vowel, when long, is nearly always obscured into *o*. Hence the Scotch, of the middle-ages as well as

---

[9]) I am, however, not quite sure if I have not, once or twice, fallen in with a *cw*, used for *wh*, in these monuments; but am not able to produce their whereabouts.

[1]) See MUNRO, A practical Grammar of the Scotch Gaëlic, p. 75.

of our days, says with broad *a:* wha (quha), wham (quham), knaw, gae, alane, stane, bane etc., whose corresponding South-English forms are: who, whom, know, go, alone, stone, bone etc., while the A. S. forms exactly agree with the first, being: wha, wham, cnawian, gán, án, stán, ban, etc.

The Scotch has further retained a pure *u* (= ou) (quite the same as the Swedish *u*) in many instances where the southern tongue has either, in different ways, obscured the ancient pronunciation, or changed the simple vowel into diphthongal sounds: doun = Engl. down, toun = Engl. town, etc. [2]):

The diphthongs are, upon the whole, much less developed in the S. E. than in the South-English. One reason of this we have already before alluded to, viz: the preservation of the gutturals. It is likely to suppose, that in the South-English the production of diphthongs took place upon these latter sounds being dropt, as a kind of compensation whereby the equilibrium was restored in the curtailed words.

When analyzing the N. A., we were aware of the complete destruction of the simple order. It is, consequently, not so much to be wondered at that its traces in the S. E. are few in number, as rather that there should be any at all. They are however, as was to be expected, very rare, scarcely more than six or seven: eghen Ps. 10, 5; sothren Br. V, 380; schoyne Br. I. 316, fone Ps. 37, 4; oxyn W. VI. 18, 244. — In works whose authors have been exposed to a Southern influence, these traces are not so uncommon as in the pure Scotch. — The S. E. form of children, is childer, of brethren, brether; children and brethren only being found in writings from the 16th century.

Although the A. S. pl. termination -as, weakened into -is (ys), is the most common, there are still, in the more ancient writings, some scarce remnants to be found of the other declensions of the Complex Order. Thus, a few traces of a gen. sg. in *e* (which might be fancied to derive from an obscure remini-

---

[2]) Ignorance of this is the cause why we often hear Scotch names clipt in an awful way.

scence of Rask's III, 2, the *a* having been softened into *e*) are met with:

wes nocht hys Fadyre Ayre W. II. pr. 8; þe sone — als lang as he is at his fadre burde Le. XIV. Athelred. Edgare þe pesybil Sowne W. VI, 15, 59; Willame Frasere Hart is layd W. VIII, 13, 15. Sometimes we see this gen. formed quite in the A. S. way: all hys Fadyr tyme W. III, 3, 158; hys Brodyr Armoure hale W. V, 3, 33. — in þi droving dai Ps. 19, 2; oure saule hele and salvacioun Kng. p. 16; kuychthede tume, ibm p. 19, — perhaps are also worth notice [3]).

The pl. of nouns that in the A. S. were of the neu. gender are tolerably often found in the pl. terminating in — *e* [4]), or like the sg. This practice extends, now and then, also to nouns, which in the A. S. were of the masc. (and fem.?) gender. In the latter case it may be accounted for by the N. A. practice of throwing off the *s* of the pl. termination -*as*. Most of the instances to be produced are also found terminating in -*is*, which, indeed, gradually excluded the other pl.: sex moneth W. I, 1, 72; thre thousand yhere W. II, pr. 7; fyve wynter W. IV, 8, 13; wike þinge Ps. 6, 9; genge fest are Ps. 9, 16; hende [5]) mine Ps. 27, 2. — In the Ps., words in -ness and -ing often take a final *e*, but it is, in most instances, impossible to make out, if it is a mark of oblique case, pl., or only a superfluous appendix.

The preceding instances are, as already observed, very rare, and it was, later, exclusively the neut. which in the A. S. were alike in sg. and pl. that kept firm against the pl. termin. -*is*. Thus some are still found in the M. S. S. of the 16th cent.:

---

[3]) Many more instances of the same kind might be easily collected, were it not for the Middle-English showing a great tendency to composition, which often makes us doubt, whether we have before us one compound word or two single ones, the one depending of the other.

[4]) Sometimes this *e* is the superfluously affixed vowel that we became acquainted with p. 26. — Respecting the pl. moneth, we observe that it must derive from a N. A. moneðo, as: Thir fische, Wal. 1, 397 from a N. A. fisco. — cf. p. 25.

[5]) Is this form of a Scandin. origin, hand not undergoing vowel-change in the A. S., but well in the Old-Norse?

Weill XIV yeir foroutin wenc Al. p. 40; ane hundreth scoir. Al. p. 10.

Nearly all substantives form their pl in -*is*, often written -*ys*, the latter vowel appearing in S. E. always to have had the same sound as *i*. We observe, that the gen. sg. terminates in the same way, and that the apostrophe is never used in g. pl. In the Ps., as well as in Syr Gawane, the common termination is *es:* þe mone and Sternes [6]) in might of night [7]) Ps. 135, 9; — þat thogt mi steppes til underga Ps. 139, 5: þat siþen depreced prowinces, & patroūes bicome G. K. 7; þe steropes G. K. 170. — North of the Tweed -*es* is only fallen in with in the writings of such authors as had a tendency to anglicize — as Knox, Hume, etc. — while all the pure Scotch stick to-*is*; þire Pápis W. V, 9, 457; þire Emperouris W. V. 9, 612; in þai Landys W. V. 2, 110; þe Saxonys and þe Scottis Blude W. VII, 3, 162; My sensis are Rob. and Mak. holtis so hair Howl. 60; the Grekis tentis Vir. p. 73, 11; their wordis Bell. f. VII; grysis thretty Vir. p. 152, 8. — This may be enough as examples of forms occurring on every page of the Scotch authors. — I am not aware of any traces of the gen. pl. in -*e* [8]) in the writings of these people.

Dr. GUEST [9]) has shown that in the South-English the adjectives only late gave up the A. S. terminations, most of them being still found in M. S. S. of the 14th century. He gives the following scheme of the indefinite declension:

---

[6]) This form seems worth a particular notice being, probably, the simple A. S. pl. steorran (N. A. stearra) with the pl. -*es*. It may, however, with as good reason, be referred to the O. Norse stjarna.

[7]) We here observe that the A. S. aspirated *h* to the south of the Tweed generally becomes *gh*, while to the north of that river it is *ch*.

[8]) Some are met with in the Ps. and in Syr Gawane, as well as in the extract given by WARTON, (ed. PRICE), II, p. 54, from a life of Alexander, written in a mongrel of South.-Engl. and S. E.

[9]) Proceed. of the Philol. Society I. p. 65.

	Sg:			*Pl.*:
	m.	f.	n.	
N.	god	god	god	gode
G.	godes	godre	godes	godre
D.	goden	godre	goden	goden
A.	godne	gode	god	gode.

These inflexions may all be found; but there is much inconsisting in the manner of using them, and that, sometimes, even in the same M. S. — In Chaucer only the inflexions in nom. and gen. pl. are encountered.

We remember from the N. A. that the indefinite declension of the adjectives was, already in the Glosses, in a state of perfect decay, chiefly depending on the dropping of *n*. We should therefore be not a little amazed, if most of those South-Engl. inflexions were found in the S. E. But in this respect it duly proves its lineage. The *n* of the dat. and acc. is never found, no more makes the fem. *r* its appearance in the gen. and dat.[1]), and I am only aware of a single adjectival gen. sg. terminating in *-is (ys)*[2]). Except in gen. pl., the S. E. adjective, in W., always ends in *e*, which, however, is often thrown away. In Barbour we once meet with an adjectival pl. in *-is*, which in his book stands quite isolated, but towards the close of the 15th century becomes somewhat more usual, as will afterwards be shown.

Respecting the defin. declension of the, adjectives we already remarked in the N. A. Glosses a certain tendency to confound it with the indefin., and in that space of time which falls between the interlining of the N. A. Glosses and the composing of the Bruce and the Oryg. Cronykil of Scotl. almost every trace

---

[1]) The only instance I remember having seen is allryn:
— to know of allryn tyme the mowence. Br. I, 134.
This form has a rather curious appearance. JAMIE., s. voc, derives it from all and the A. S. rinnan, but I think nobody will believe him. — In particles it is sometimes retained: anerly, alanerly.

[2]) A burgess may thruch his anerys (?!) voyce put hym till athe Le. XXVIII. Hither we may perhaps also refer: Quhen Willame-Reddis dayis ware dwne. W. VIII, 6, 30.

of it has disappeared³). It is, indeed, only *self*⁴) that still retains the terminating *n*, which Guest (l. c.) has very judiciously pointed out to derive from the circumstance of this adject., in A. S., when combined with the person. pron., being often used in the defin. forms instead of the indefin. ones. — Ex. to be given under the pronouns.

We think it superfluous to give evidence of *e* being used as a termination of the adject. in the sg. as well as in the pl., coincident as it is with the common practice of Chaucer and his contemporaries. The room won by this restriction we shall appropriate to a more ample account of the gen. pl. and the peculiar nom. pl. — At first, we remark that the gen. termination is only found in adject. following the gen. pl. of the pers. pronouns⁵):

— trouch thar aller hale assent. Br. I, 137. And right so by theire aller dome S. S. l. 2828.

This ancient form of the gen. is, however, very seldom fallen in with. The Scotch writers of the 15th and 16th centuries more often add to it the genitival ending -is:

— ordanyt wyth þaire allaris Will. W. VIII, 35, 178; owre alleris offence Vir. p. 406; thar allaris Howl. LVII.

A little before, we adverted to the occurrence of a pl. in *-is*. The first instance of this to be found, is, I think:

— off ryngis with rich stanys That war off knychtis fyngyris taneys, Br. II, 604⁶).

---

³) In the South-English many more are found; see Guest, l. c.
⁴) It may, however, be that samyn, a word of frequent occurrence, derives its *n* from the same source: -in the samyn tym Br. I. 252.
⁵) See some more instances, quoted from Syr Tristrem, p. 57. — Ch. uses it in the same way:
And yit this manneiple sette here aller cappe l. 588; Schal han a soper at your alther cost l. 801.
⁶) Innes, in his ed. of the Brus, reads: stane — tane; which Barbour undoubtedly *could* have written. But although the pl. in *-is* be not met with in the much older M. S. of Wynt., at least in that portion published by M'Pherson, I think that, in the passage quoted from Br., its occurrence cannot be owing to the circumstance of the copy we possess of thiswork having been transcribed about 1480. It will,

In the M. S. S. from the latter half of the 15th cent. this plur. becomes more and more usual, and in those from the following this termination is used promiscuously with that in -e. the unworthy cowartis Knychtis that fleis in batailis. Kng. p. 21. — the ordour of Knychthede, suld — — accorde to the properties corporalis, and personalis as spiritualis ibm p. 32 [7]). — we hawe sight spirituale — — and all Goddis workis uisibilis and invisibilis ibm p. 45: be experience of utheris authoris, Bel. proheme: — ane cumpany of siclik young men fugitivis as he wes ibm fol. 1.

Most frequently we find this termination added to the past. part. of say:

þe saidis lyneris sall Le. CV. þir forsaidis thyngis Le. CXVI. — thare the saidis thre Persouns within the said Get, ressavit the saids twa charges, quhilks, Col. II. p. 166. — This inflection long kept its ground in the language of Law and Ceremony [8]).

---

indeed, be shown that Wynt. added this ending to the pron. quhilk, when it referred to a plural substantive.

[7]) With this we may compare: — — losse of oure goodes temporales, Ch. p. 151, A.

[8]) GUEST (l. c.) is of opinion that this curious inflection has its ground in the writers' propensity to imitate the inflection of the French and Latin adject. The French has, no doubt, influenced the S. E, but it is not probable that it has given rise to this practice. There is, indeed, an indigenous cause, lying at hand to produce it.' It has been pointed out by Dr. GUEST himself, although he appear not to have been aware of its consequence for the explanation of the adjectival pl. in -is. It was, in the 14th and following cent., not unusual to qualify one substantive by another, the qualifying substant. always following the one qualified. Chaucer, as well as Wicliffe, very often make use of this construction, and there are still some phrases preserved in the modern English that must be ranged under this class of idioms. Such are: Knights-Templars; Knights-Hospitallers: Friars-Minors, etc.

This practice was common also to the Scotch writers: — come — — with — — and servandis Grekis and Egiptianis, Bel. fol. 1. Quhen the vignerounes labouraris had wrouht all the day Kng. p. 51. — When the substantive in this way had encroached upon the adject., it is very natural, that a confusion of adject. and subst. should

The pronouns of the S. E. exhibit many discrepancies from the corresponding ones found in the South-English writings of the 14th and 15th centuries. Curious enough, the S. E. pronouns agree in many points with those of modern English, while those of Middle-South-English much more closely correspond with the A. S. practice; — still a proof of the forwardness of the dialect of the North in point of linguistical development.

The pron. personal of I and II do not command a particular attention, as they throughout agree with the South-English [3]). We shall therefore with respect to them only remark: that *you* is in the Scotch writers never [1]) used as a nom. pl. the regular *ye* always being maintained in its ancient right [2]). and that *the* is, twice or thrice, found for thou:

Ga hens [3]). the Scot. the mekill dewill the speid. Wal. II, 93; Thow sall nocht de the allane. Howl. XL.

ensue, in consequence of which the termination of the subst. was added to the adject.

[9]) In an extract from Wint. in SIBBALD'S Chronicle of Scottish Poetry, we find *a* for I. The devil says to St. Serf:

I ken þau art a connand clerk;
to which the saint replies:
Gif a swa be —

In M'PHERSON's ed. it runs: Gywe I swa be, W. V, 12, 1244. — As far as I know, only one M. S. of The Orygynale Cronykil of W., that one preserved in the Advocates' Library, at Edinburgh, is to be found. It is, therefore, probable that the reading of Sibbald is only a misreading — his texts being generally very bad, and not the least to be relied upon. — I have nowhere in Scotch writings, whether ancient or modern, found this form of the I pron. pers., which, if I am not mistaken, only is current in some of the provincial dialects of England.

[1]) In pure Scotch I have only once found ye used with preposit.: Gif þi maill man pay ye nocht — · — · it is rycht leyfull to ye to take pundis. Le. LIII.

[2]) Concerning the English pronouns person., and the changes they have undergone, the reader is referred to Dr. GUEST's fine paper, Proceed. of the Phil. Soci. I. p. 277.

[3]) As we shall have no opportunity to speak of the particles in the text, some remarks will incidentally be given in the notes, when our examples present forms worth noticing. — Hens (= E. Hence)

Respecting the pron. of III pers., we observe that, in sg., *he* has had least to suffer, only having lost the acc., hine, in the place of which the dat., him, has stept in. This change appears to have been brought about very early, for neither in the Ps. nor in any of the other Scotch writings I have fallen in with it. *Heo*, retained in the South-English romances, in Syr Gawane, and Sir Tristrem, (in these works probablyo wing to their having been transcribed in the South of England), but, as far as I am aware of, out of use with Chaucer, is never found in the S. E., which has substituted the demonst. seo, by the Scotch always written: scho. for it. Passages where it occurs will be given under the verbs. It has, further, cast away the acc. hi (N. A. hia, hea), for which the dat. is used. — *It*, in S. E., is seldom spelled: hit, as in the South-E. — The neut. gen., his, I cannot with full certainty affirm to have found:

Causis the cirth his fruits till express, Pal. pr. VIII [4]).

Respecting this example I must remark: that if the question were of a personification of the earth (which, not having the book at hand, I cannot now make out), the Latin-bred Douglas would never have put the masc. His, if the true reading, must be neut. But as the edition from which I quote this same example is an exceedingly bad one, it is far from being certain that it is not a mere printing-fault. — In Vir., however, we find some instances where his really appears to be used in the neut. gender:

Amyd the cite stude ane semly schaw
With hys maist plesand sobir schaddowis —
Vir. p. 49, 8.

and words of the same formation are very scarce, the ancient A. S. forms hyne etc. being of regular occurrence. Hence, thence etc. are South-English, and imported into Scotland, where they make their appearance towards the end of the 15th century.

[4]) Of the two following instances the former seems to be a personification, the other a constructio ad synesin:

The burning maist ambitious breist wald quite his noble fame. —
- — — - . the little childe —
Casts downe his face. — Hm. p. 27.

Thar is a place quham the Grekis, thai say,
Onto hys name clepis Hesperia.
Vir. p. 54, 23.

Nocht for our tung is in the selwyn skant,
Bot for that I the fowth of langage want,
Quhar as the cullour of his properte
To kepe the sentens tharto constrenyt me
Vir. p. 7, 7.

The first instance of the gen. *its* I have met with is:
Ane vther cans siclike I wait ye ken
For to bring but its Ill thats not thair ben. S. S. pr.

In W., and the writers of the 15th cent., it is never found; these even very seldom use *it* with prepositions. Among the few examples I have found are:
— gude justis begynnis at it selfe, Kng. p. 24.
— in itself, ibm p. 30. — in it. Ps. 117, 20.

Commonly *the* [5]), in such constructions, is used in its stead:
þe swn — —
Is in the self bath lycht and clere. W. VIII, 37. 87.
And day be day fra all vertew decrest
Continuallie the self it ay opprest. S. S. p. 2.
Thay said the case that we can schaw to you
Into the self is wonder sorrowfow. S. S. p. 25.
— quhilk injust regiment is of the selfe fals. Kng. p. 49.

Of the A. S. pl. of this pron. — hi, hira, him — pretty well preserved in the South-English romances, and, partly, still in Chaucer, there is not a trace to be found in the Ps., and the writings to the north of the Tweed. This we had to expect from the very marked tendency of the N. A. to substitute forms of the demonstrative þaet, ðe, ðiu for the ancient pron. of the third person. It seems probable that this practice may be ascribed to the Scandinavian influence; the Northern tongue, as far as historically known, always having used forms of the demonstr. þat, sa, su, for the wanting neut. sg. and the pl. of the pron.

---

[5]) It is difficult to decide, if *the* here is to be considered a remnant of the demonstrat. þe of the N. A., or only as the defin. article, self then being used substantively.

of the third person. We have, however, already adverted to the circumstance of the same substitution being used in the O. Friesian.

The following examples are chosen in such a way as to show the different modes of spelling the forms of this pron [6]):

Genge fest are in forward þat þai made;
In þis snare whilke þai hid swa
Gripen es þe fote of þa. Ps. 9, 16.
Ses ton — —
þat in þi hende þaw gyve þaim non, Ps. 9, 35.
And he gaf þam in hend of genge ma,
And laverdes ere of þas þat hated þa. Ps. 105, 41.
In to þai landis þat þai wan. W. II, 10, 40.
Ane of þai W. II, 8, 20.
Hys Bropir he slwe, and syn all þa
þat he conth trow. W. III, 3, 125.
— eftyre þa þis Etoyr gat. W. II, 10, 90.
All þai he had corrumpyd þan
Wyth gret gyftis, þan þat he
Hys accusatowris trowyd to be. W. VI, 14, 20.
— tretyd þe Scottis favorably,
And þame defendyd manlyly. W. VI, 8, 25.
Mak we four bataillis of tha. Br. VIII, 285.
Mony gud man — — in till thai rowtis
men mycht se. Br. IX, 16.
— — Inglis suld þe Scottis prys,
And þai þaim on the samyn wys. W. VIII, 35, 179.

We see from these examples that the dat. was in course of supplanting the ancient acc., but had not yet won a complete victory. I think, however, that the acc. þa does not occur in any other works than the two quoted.

---

[6]) It is not unlikely that the S. E. practice was the cause of hi etc. being done away with in the South-English. — For it is well known that the literary productions of the North, in many respects superior to those of the South — which, until the time when Chaucer turned the balance, were, one and all, translations from the French — had a large public in the South.

Respecting the reflect. pron. formed with self, we have not here space for a full discussion of all the interesting questions connected with the origin of such forms as: thyself, myself etc. of the present English. We hope in coming years to be able to treat this matter at large, having to that end collected a great number of passages from S. E. as well as from South-English authors. — We shall, therefore, here only give a few instances showing forth the S. E. forms of these reflect.:

Hymself come þare W. VIII. 35. 70. þa wyst na Rede till [7]) help þame — selwyn W. V, 9. 588. — be þame self W. V. 10. 1286. — syk evill men as thame self Kng. p. 34. — bot be thame selvyn twane Vir. p. 195, 15. — thi selvyn ibm p. 205. — Kan not hymselvyn hyde ibm p. 184, 6. — The other pron. are formed in quite the same way. — Pl. in-*es*, do not occur, or but very solitarily, until the time of Knox, when this termination began to supersede the ancient ones.

Passing to the possessive pron., we remark that they are the same as in the present English [8]). We shall therefore not make a stay to account for their forms; whereas some other peculiarities in their use call for attention. In A. S. some possessive pron. were declined as indefin. adject., while others (the gen. of the third person) were used unchanged. The ancient practice, although of course not without confusion, was kept up in the dialects originated in the A. S. Thus, we generally find min. thin. owr. yhour, when combined with subst. in pl., taking the plural -*e*. But already in the period of decay of the A. S. the inflection of the possess. proved yet more progressive, when the

---

[7]) Here we observe that *till* is by W. more often used before the infint. than *to;* in the other Scotch authors the one is found as often as the other.

[8]) My and thy, often spelled mi (mi occurs in the Leg.; þe domen of mi kinedom p. 78), thi, are of frequent occurrence in the Ps. and W. — What is the origin of these two possessives — wanting in A. S.? Are they the Gaëlic mo (my), do (thy); or the curtailed min, þin (here we remark the N. A. tendency to drop the *n*), or, originally, the dat. me, þe (it may be fancied that the dat. personal, in the lapse of time, has become a poss.)? — In every case, it is certain that the present diphthongal sound of *y* is of later growth.

genit. of the third person were more and more considered as adjectives, and, consequently, used with adjectival terminations. In the Legend of St. Kath. from Alex. we read:

    to þe temple, in þe tun
    of hise heaðene godes. p. 4.
    Porphire and alle hise. p. 121.
    — hise Lerning cnihhtess Orm. 1. 17820.
    Swiftly rennes sagh hisse. Ps. 147, 15.

This form has however become obsolete in the Scotch authors, at least am I not aware of its occurring in any one of those I have had opportunity of perusing. This is very natural, as the *e* more and more lost its quality of termination.

We have still to mention the practice of imparting the termination -*is* to the possess. pron., and in this way to produce a double inflection, of the same kind as in some adjectives already mentioned. — In the earliest writings these pronouns are used absolutely in the same forms as they have, when determining substantives. But the double inflection is also found very early, and its use seems dependent on the same want of determination, which has produced analogous phenomena in the German and Scandinavian languages [9]). — A few examples may suffice:

    All hale my Landis sall yhowris be. W. VIII, 18. 79.
    þe Victory ay þairis was. W. VIII. 27. 190.
    But magre þairris ibm 38. 197.
    Bot oþir Lordis, þat war by,
    Sayd he had fillyd fullyly
    His Baggis, and þairris tume war ibm 40. 93.

Thus, all the other possess. that in present English have the same forms.

---

[9]) Cf. the Sw. deras, dessas; the Germ. dessen, deren. — The last inflection, probably originating in the defin. declens. of the A. S. adject., is, according to Dr. GUEST (l. c. p. 69) also found in Wicliffe's translation of the Bible:

    —— the kingdom of hevenes is herun Mt. 5. —- and some of ouren wenten to the grane Luc. 24. -— and still in use among the lower classes of the English people: his'n, her'n, their'n.

Of the A. S. demonstr. pronouns, þaet, se, seo, has best retained its forms in modern English. Still it has lost considerably, and that already in the most ancient monuments. Se and seo have disappeared as demonst.; the former never more to be seen, the latter, as scho ¹), overtaking the part of the lost pron. pers. hio, the oblique cases of which continued being used, while those of seo became antiquated. The pl. serves in W. and the P's. both as demonst. and as pron. pers. Towards the end of the 15th century the former application appears gradually to have been given up ²). — The introduction of they, as pron. pers., in the South-English may with reason be assigned to a Northern influence; for had it in South-England originally been applied as pron. pers. it would probably have been spelled tho. — in þai dayis W. V, 8. 231; Kyng wes in þá ³) landis W. IV. 8. 40; And be mon at queme sal þa speches P's. 18, 5. — And of tha wordis quhilkis the goddis gan say Vir. p. 137, 19; Tha landis quhilkis were for ws provyde Vir. p. 150, 21; thaye dayis Kng. p. 34; Bel. fol. 3; with part of thay landis Bel. f. 1. — A. A. l. 315, we read: The wynde and the wedyrs þane welkin in hydis: where þane, in all probability, is the old acc. masc. I have thought it worth noticing here, as the verse has quite a Scotch contenance.

The other demonst., þis, þes, þeos, has given up the two latter forms, and uses this for all genders, quite as in the South-English. Its plur., þas ⁴). (the spelling those is undoubtedly of

¹) We remember from the N. A. that sio very seldom occurs in the Gl. It is therefore rather somewhat curious to find it, in the S. E., instead of hio; the N. A. practice inducing us to expect a word deriving from ðio.

²) It is however (see the examples), now and then, fallen in with in the writings of the 16th cent.

³) In the South-English this þa — in conformity with the common practice of changing A. S. á into o — has become þo: — sle all tho children Dig. p. 7; for I do enermore þo þingis. Wic. Job. 8. In this form it is sometimes found in the S. E.: He wore one of tho Cl. II. 164. — It is also met with in G. K. and A. A., and is everywhere a sure sign of Southern influence.

⁴) We think it not quite out of place here to make a remark on the formation of the Engl. *these*, although this form be wanting in the

a Southern origin) was scarcely current in S. E. Traces of inflection, except the final *e*, are never met with. Thas occurs in the Ps.:

|as |at in me rises nou
Schent mote |.ai be. Ps. 108, 28.
And laverdes ere of |,as |at hated |,a Ps. 105, 41.

but in all S. E. authors, whose language has not been worked upon by the Southern dialects, I am not aware of it.[5]). The dialect has in thir a pronoun which always is used for thas as well as for these:

all thir fowlis Howl. V. ilkane of |ire wes crownyd Kyng W. VII, 3, 38. For mony of |ir Kyngis lyis W. VI, 19, 59. Of |ire Papys successywe W. V, 9, 456. Thir commodites quhilkis ar Bel. ch. V. — The examples show that it also takes a final *e* [6]).

Neither in the N. A. nor in the W. S. there is anything corresponding to this pronoun, and the explanation of Chalmers

———

strictly speaking Scotch authors. This was in the South-English very early treated as his, that is to say, it was inflected by adding a final *e* (see WHITE'S ed. of Ormul. I. 158, 170, 331, etc.), to the influence of which the long *e* of these probably is to be ascribed. We must, however, observe, that *e* is affixed also when it does not determine a substantive in pl.:

þat sent his speche til erthe |isse.
Swiftly rennes sagh hisse. Ps. 147, 15

and that it is left out even when this is the case: |is |ingis Wicl. Joh. 8. — With other writers we find it spelled in different ways, but in general so as to note the length of its vowel. Wicl. himself often writes it: |es, and in other writers it is spelled: thys, theis, etc., with or without a final *e*.

[5]) Those made, however, in the 16th cent. such inroads upon the S. E. that it is found even in Lindesay, who, in my opinion, is one of the purest Scotch writers that exist, and throughout keeps his promise:

Quharefore to coilearis, carteris and to cukis,
To Jok and Thom my ryme sall be direckit;
With cunnyng men howbeit it will be lackit.

[6]) I am not aware of this word in the Ps.; it occurs in G. G. and A. A., but not in G. K. — see the Gloss. affixed to Sir Fred. MADDEN'S Syr Gawayne.

(see p. 56) being unacceptable, it is, I think, necessary to admit of its importation from Scandinavia, where we precisely find the pl. þeir closely agreeing wit þir of the S. E.

The interrog. and the rel. pronoun are in the S. E. the same as in the South-English, the difference being referrible to the differences of vowel-change and consonant-dropping already accounted for p. 60. At the same occasion we have mentioned the Scotch practice of substituting *quh* for *wh* [7]). The A. S. wha, what, consequently become: quha, quhat, with a long and broad *a*. Forms with *o* occur in anglicizing authors.

The use of the relative quhilk has some peculiarities very characteristic of the dialect. It becomes quhilkis, when it refers to a plural or collective substantive. The first instance of this practice is:

Contenand hale thre thowsand yhere
Nyne scowre and foure ourpassyt clere
The qhuilkys as Orosius
Intyl his Cornyclis tellys us. W. II. pr. 9.

In W. it is, however, very seldom inflected. But towards the end of the 15th century the practice becomes more and more general [8]), and in the works of the 16th it is nearly a rule:

All broustaris þe quhilkis sellis ale — — and all hukstaris þe quhilkis byis and sellis. Le. LXVII [9]). Na man aw to be hingyt for les price þan for twa sheeip of the quhilkis ilkane is worth XVI de. A. R. W. XIII. The quhilkis was excusit to

---

[7]) This pronunciation is still to be heard in the streets of Edinburgh.

[8]) In the Howl it is never inflected, and in the Br. and Wal. but sparingly. In Dunbar, Douglas, Bel., Lindsay, etc. nearly throughout.

[9]) Assise Regis Willelmi, IX, stands: - sa that he will nocht cum to jugement, his lord of þe qhuilkis he haldis sall tak. — GUEST, I think in Phil. Proceed., I, has remarked that the preposition of in the Mid. English sometimes governs a gen. This seems to be the case here. I have fallen in with a not inconsiderable number of similar constructions, which I hope in coming days to get an opportunity of publishing along with a good deal of other observations on the S. E. as well as the South-English.

nocht laboure Kng. p. 12. Facund epistillis quilks quhilum
Ovid wrait. Pal. II. 5. Grant that these instruments of shame
Quhilks dayly do offend. Hm. p. 4.
Quhilkis charteris war gravyn in merbyll. Bel. f. IX.
Before leaving the pronouns we give a few passages where
at (see p. 54) occurs as a relat.:

I the defy, power and all the laiff
At helpis the her, off thi fals natioun. Wal. VI, 380.
Rycht weill he trowit — —
It was sum dewill at sic malice began. Wal. V, 199.
— fre wyll to do
That at hys hart hym drawis to Br. I. 247.

For more examples see JAMIES. Diction., under at.

We now pass on to make an account of the S. E. verbs.
We observe at the first glance that they are true descendants
of the O. N. Anglic.. but, ol course, have undergone considerable
changes, and lost a good deal of what in that dialect they did
still possess. The Complex Order exhibits many peculiarities in
which it differs from the South-English. and is well worth the
attention of the philologist. But, as the space of our dissertation is very limited, we must confine ourselves to producing
some few of them in a note. without even being able to give
them in all the requisite forms [1]). The tendency of these verbs

[1]) byde	—	bad (baid)	—	—
(break)		brak	—	—
creip	—	crap	—	—
climb	—	clamb	—	clumben
cum	—	com	—	cumyn
can	—	couth (could)	—	
fynd	—	fand	—	fwndyn
ga	—	(yhode)	—	gayne
get	—	gat	—	gotlyn
let	—	luit	—	—
(leap)	—	lap	—	—
lyg	—	lay	—	—
reif	—	raif	—	—
ryde	—	rade	—	

to pass over into the Simple Order, which we observed in the Glosses, has however not been dormant during the long interval of time that falls between the redaction of the North-Anglic Glosses and the composition of the earliest S. E. writings. We can no more give a complete account of these recruits of the Simple Order. But we remark that a good number of verbs, which in Chaucer, and other South-English writers, in the 14th and 15th centuries, still retain their strong conjugation, in the S. E. are used as belonging to the Simple Order. As example of this transformation the following verbs, taken from Ps. 17, may serve:

umgriped me weeles of quede (A. S. gripan, grap) v. 5.
Fra face of wicked þat twinged me swa v. 9.
He helded heuens, and doune come he (A. S. healdan, heold) v. 10.
þai onfanged me als lioun v. 12.
In heringe of ere me boghed he (A. S. bugan, beah) v. 45.
Outen sones to me lighed þai (A. S. liegan, laeg) v. 46.

It may, however, be remarked that the Ps. in this respect goes still farther than the Scotch. —

The two A. S. substantive verbs wesan and beon, N. A. wosa and bian, have, in modern English, both lost their existence in their own right, and coalesced to one word. In the language of the Middle-Ages this has already taken place, although not so completely as later. From the Scotch authors I cannot give any instances of *wosa* occurring in the subj. pres., imperat., infin., and participles. We observe that *is* occurs not only in III pres. indic., but also in the pl. [2]):

quak	—	quouke	—	—
(swear)	—	swar(swour)	—	—
(strive)	—	strave	—	—
smyte	—	smate	—	—
tyte(to lose)	—	tyt	—	—
wade	—	woud	—	—
walkyn	—	wok	—	—
will	—	wald	—	—
(write)	—	wrayt	—	—
wyn	—	wan	—	wonnyn
(yield)	—	yhald	—	—

[2]) Methinks I have also met with it used in II sg., and according

Sen your mindis is to have ane person. Bel. f. III. —
At ane eb se the Scottish is on thaym gayne Wal. VI, 1072.
his falowis that now is Kng. p. 31. Wyth wisdome and wyliness thay wirk and is as laith thair honestie to tine S. S. p.
135. Mony divers thyngis now here is Y. M.

In the same way, and quite in accordance with the genius
of the dialect, we find *was* (*wes*) used:

The Inglismen was off the toune cummande Wal. V, 12.
Quhat worthy lordis thar was Howl. XXIV.

The common plurals, however, are *are* and *war*. — The *are*
of modern English is, without any doubt, imported from the S.
E., as this plur. occurs nowhere in the W. S., is not found in
the earlier Middle-English writings, and, compared with *ben*, is
but sparingly used by Chaucer, where he does not expressly
imitate the Northern dialect, which sometimes is the case.

The only forms of *be*, which I consider as pure Scotch are
beis, pres. and imperat., the apocopated *be*, the part. pres. *beand*
and past *bein*. The form *bein* (spelled in different ways) although found in Cl., and other works of the same kind, is undoubtedly South-English, as the formation of a pres. pl. in -*n*,
as will soon be shown, is totally unknown to the Scotch proper. Beis and be are used for all persons, in both numbers,
and generally convey a future sens [3]).

He askyt leyff with thar lywis to ga
Wallace denyit, and said it beis nocht sa. Wal. IX, 1846.
Ye have [4]) me laid to sleip or it be nicht. Cl. I, 768.
For will ye are in this estait, perfay,
Sir, ye be seikand aventuris ay. Cl. I. 835.
This day for in faith he beis nocht socht. Wal, 434.

---

to GARNETT, Philol. Essays, p. 72, it is in Yorkshire presently used
for all persons of the sg.

[3]) I leave to the decision of the grammarians, if this, in a certain degree, is not still the case with be in modern Engl. Some grammarians, at least, never permit its being used, when the sense to be
expressed is not a future one. Cf. HARRISON, The Rise, Progress, and
present Structure of the English Language, p. 279.

[4]) Have is undoubtedly a Southern form, the true Scotch being:
hes. — .

Fyrst I protest, beau Schirris, be your leif,
Beis weill avisit my wark or yhe reproif. Vir. p. 6, 25.
Bath the parties beand personally present, —
the lordis auditoris decretis — quot. JAMIES. s. beand.
Thir wourdis beand said ibm.

Not being able to give an account of the other S. E. auxiliaries, as this would take up to much place, the subject being both rich and interesting, we pass on to the regular verbs.

A tendency to throw off the derivative vowels was already observed in the N. A. Its work is done in the S.-E. so that there is not a trace left of these vowels, but there reigns a uniformity as complete as ruin can effect it.

The I pres. ind. terminated, in N. A., in a vowel; this vowel, changed into *e*, is often retained, but as often dropt. Such is also the case in the South-English, and we therefore consider it quite superfluous to produce examples in order to prove that it existed in the S. E. Sometimes, however, this person takes the same termination, -*is*, as the others:

I askis help Howl. IX; whilk was hir awin varlat — as I thinkis Cl. II. 212; I set — — and spekis as I lernyt Vir. p. 6, 27; Syn I defend and forbiddis every wight Vir. p, 12, 21.

is occurs throughout in II sg. pres. ind:

Thow Scot to quhom takis thow this thing. Wal. I, 85;
Thinks thow no schaym. Wal. VIII, 399;

The III pers. always ends in the same way:

Thair standis into the sycht of Troy ane ile Vir. p. 72, 15; but in the anglicizing authors — Douglas, Knox, Hume, etc. — we very often fall in with -*th*.

The pl. ends, in all pers., in -*is:* We castis ws evir till othir besyness Wal. I, 434;

Sum grathis fast the thak and rufe of tre;
And sum about delvys the fowsy deip:
Sum chesis officeris the lawys for to kepe. Vir. p. 48, 10.
And mortal weris contempnys and comptes nocht,
Belewis weill yit than, and have in thocht. Vir. p. 55, 13.
All men spekis of my crueltie. Cl. II. 152.

This pl., the more full pl. termination of the A. S. in *að*, of the N. A. in *-as* (*es*) is — there written *-eth* [5]) — also found in the Middle-English. But beside this pl., it had another in *en*, probably grown out of a confusion of indic. and subjunct. This pl. we find sometimes used by S. E. authors, but never by the true Scotch; whereas it frequently occurs in A. A. and G. G., and seems to be a rule in G. K. and Syr Tristrem. I dare not, however, assert, that in those works it is throughout a consequence of their having been transcribed in the South of England. For this pl. termination is, indeed, also current in the Ps.:

Noght þat wickness wirken ai
In his waies yhoden þai. 118, 3.
Bot we þat liven, Laverd we blisse. 113. 18.
þat dreden Laverd. saye þai. 117. 4.

In every case, it is to be remembered, that in the N. A. Glosses the pl. subj. pres. never terminates in *-n*, but in a vowel.

Besides their taking the termination *-is*, we often find the verbs, in III sg. as well as pl., without any termination at all. In what concerns the pl., this practice — agreeing with the practice of modern English — derives from the A. S. apocopated pl. termination. Methinks two examples may suffice:

Eftyre him dar na man ga. Br. II, 561.
We lyff into sa mekill dreid. Br. II. 710.

Respecting the vowel-termination of the subj. pres. I dare not affirm anything for sure. For the affixing and dropping of the final *e* are not bound to any fixed rules. Besides, we see in S. E. as in modern English, the indic. constantly used, even when a contingency is implied. For this reason, it is nearly

---

[5]) This termination, softened into *-es*, is still current among the lower classes of the English people. I remember having seen, in some work of Dickens' or Bulwer's, a boots expressing himself: we takes in the Times, but they takes in the Morning Star; a mode of expression which, in an historical point of view, is quite as correct as the use of the apocopated A. S. pl.

always impossible to make out, if we have a subj. or only a not inflected indic. before us.

The pret. indic. terminates in the Ps. always in -ed, and in W. often in -yde (= ide):

Dydo fyrst gert formyd he
And wallyd welle þat gryte cytè;
Hyr gudame lufyde Eneas; W. III. 3. 165.

(See also the quotations from W. already given in the preceding).

In Bruce and Wallace -t [6]) has been substituted for d: the vowel being generally i (y):

And thar schip thai lychtyt sone:
And rowyt syn with all thar mycht;
And scho, that swa wes maid lycht,
Raykyt slidand throw the se. Br. III, 90.

This termination has always kept its ground in the Scotch, and continues still being used. — II sg. terminates in -is:

— thow hechtis till hyng me. Wal. V, 750.

But generally it is used without termination:

The barde worth brane wod, and bitterly couth ban,
How Corby messinger. quoth he, with sorrow now syngis,
Thow ischit out of Noyes ark, and to the erd wan.
Taryit as a traytour, and brocht [6]) na tythingis. Howl. LXIII.

In the quotation given a little before, from Br., we saw that the preter. indic. has the same form in sg. as in pl., the termination -en of the Middle-South-English being entirely unknown to the Scotch proper. From the N. A. Glosses, there was reason to suppose that this also would be the case in Northumberland. But in the Ps. pret. are found terminating in -en: In his waies yhoden þai. Ps. 118, 3. Those instances, however, are very rare, and in general the pret. behaves in the Ps. in the true Scotch way. — The preter. subj. falls together with the indic. —

---

[5]) Concerning this t, we refer to the instances, given p. 22, of the same consonant occurring in the weak past part. of the N. A.

[6]) In the same way, the strong verbs invariably stick to the A. S practice.

The terminations of the imperat. are to be seen in the following passages:
Harkis. Ladies. your bewte was the caws;
Harkis, knychtis, the wod fury of Mart;
Wys men, attendis mony sorofull claws;
And ye dyssavoris, reid heir your proper art. Vir. p. 71, 15;
Consider it warly. reid oftar than anys. Vir. p. 6, 25;
He said grymeand (?) hyngis and drawys. Br. III, 550;
Tharfor, he said, atour all thing
Kepys you fra disparyng. Br. II, 594.

The imperat. terminat. -*is* is the A. S. -*að*, N. A. -*as*, with the *a* softened into *i*.

Respecting the infin. of the S. E. verbs, we observe that, agreeing with the practice of the N. A. Glosses, it throughout wants the final *n* [7]). Of the gerund, still found in the Glosses, there is not a trace left in the Scotch works. In the Ps. there are one or two instances to be found:

Alle blis of him to biginne,
Doghtres of kinges fra withinne. Ps. 44, 14.

The gerund was to be dispensed with, but a partic. present no language can do without, and should it, in one way or another, happen to disappear there must be provided a substitute to fill up the vacant office. Thus, the South-English, having slighted the ancient A. S. part. pres. in — *ende*, was forced to have recourse to the verbal nouns in -*ing*. These are, indeed, already in Layamon's Brut used for the true part. pres. [8]). In the dialect north of the Humber, the A. S. partic., here, in accordance with the N. A. Glosses, written — *and*, sturdily kept its ground, and, as will be shown, even encroached upon the territory of the derivatives in -*ing*.

We give some instances of its occurring in Scotch works of the 15th and 16th anturies:

[7]) Three or four instances of -n in the infin. may, however, be quoted from the Ps. and the Scotch authors. — Concerning the disappearing of the gerund cf. Sir F. MADDEN, Layamon's Brut, I. p. XLIX.

[8]) Cf. Sir F. MADDEN l. c. p. LI. - Some information about this matter may also be had in HORNE TOOKE'S Diversions of Purley, (ed. 1860). p. XXXIX.

And thiggand and pouer am I Ps. 39, 18;
Sextene yhere he wes lyvand W. VI, 8. 20;
Raykyt slidand throw the se Br. III, 93;
The scherand snerd glaid to the colar bane. Wal. I, 414;
Thai apperit — — fair farrand and fre Howl. XII;
Throw skaldand fyr ay as thay skippit Db. Dance;
All birnand full of bricht stonis deir Cl. 1, 24.
Thai delvand fand. Vir. p. 49, 12.

These may suffice to prove the existence of this form during the mentioned time. — In the South-English it died away very early, and is only exceptively fallen in with in Chaucer.

As examples of the practice to put the part. in -and instead of verbal nouns in -ing, the following may serve:

And al þine offrand mined he Ps. 19, 2; Offres offrand of rightwisnesse Ps. 4, 6 tythandis Howl. XI; Br. IV. 747; — maid gud sembland [9]) for to fycht Br. VI, 711; Till slepand men that walkand was nocht soft Wal. VII, 440.

But the nouns in -ing did not fail to take their revenge on the participles for this encroachment. From the South, they came on accoutred as part. pres., and the ancient participle was soon borne down, however, not without gallantly defending every inch of its ground. In the Ps., W., Br., Wal., Howl., not the least trace of it is to be found; in Kng. a single one: the hewing ax p. 23. But in the same degree we advance in time, the instances go on continually increasing. With Douglas and Dunbar the part. in -ing are yet inferior in number to the true ones. In Bel. it is already the inverse, and in the works of Knox and Hume I do not think it possible to pick up a single part. in-*and*. It is done away with in the Broad Scotch of the present day, whose part. pres. in-*in*, no doubt, is identical with -ing.

Before laying down our pen, and, for a time at least, taking leave of the Scotch dialect, we may be permitted to set forth some final reflexions on our subject. — We have shown that the North-Anglic, as it is preserved in the monuments we

---

[9]) This rather reminds of the French phrase: faire semblant.

possess, was, in many respects, differing from the West-Saxon. We have, further, tried to show that this diversity was not the consequence of Scandinavian settlements in the North of England, but depending on a cause lying deeper than in an external influence. — We have, further, seen that the S. E. dialect is the true descendant of the N. A., and that it bears on it all characteristic marks of the latter, due allowance made for changes which a development, or, if you like it more, a decay of some centuries had carried along with it, and, from an internal necessity, inherent in all languages, must carry along with it. — The true period of the S. E., as a literary dialect, falls in the 14th and 15th centuries; the purest specimens of it are the Ps. and W. In Br. and Wal., the Howl. and Kng., it had already taken up some scraps from the Southern tongue. This is very natural, and is to be explained, partly, by the custom of the Scotch clerks of repairing to the English Universities, partly, from the rise of Chaucer, who to more Scotsmen than Douglas was:

"— — venerabill Chauser principal poët but peir,
Hevenly trumpat, orlege, and reguler,
In eloquens balmy, cyndyt and dyall,
Mylky fontane, cleir strand, and roys ryall —"

whom every wight had the right to imitate and rob. Particularly, we see that his influence has been great with Douglas, who even, in a certain degree, acknowledges his obligations to the Southern tongue, "where the Scottis wes scant."

Thus, we find him repeatedly make use of the prefix y- in the past part., although this is totally unknown to Ps., W., and the true Scotch authors. — Chaucer, however, had much earlier begun to destroy the S. E. James I was an ardent client of his, and particularly the Kings Quair, swarming with Anglicisms as it is, can scarcely be considered a Scotch poem [1]). But the encroachments of the Southern speech proceeded on a still larger scale in the latter portion of the 16th century. If the

---

[1]) At all events, it is a pity that the lovers of Middle-English poetry do not possess a good edition of the works of James I. — I hope, however, that my honoured friend Dr. J. A. CARLYLE will soon publish the edition he for some years has been preparing.

Anglicisms are rare in Dunbar, Douglas, and Bellenden, the Scotticisms are rare in the works of Knox, Hume, and others; and Scotland had during this time scarcely more than one eminent literary character who wrote a language that has only a slight sprinkling of English. Only for that reason, he would have deserved Sir WALTER SCOTT's rescue from an oblivion into which he undeservedly had fallen:

"Still is thy name in high account
And still thy verse has charms,
Sir David LINDESAY of the Mount,
Lord Lion King-at-arms!"

Still there were books printed in Scotch, but these were all of an inferior value as literary productions. — Characteristic enough, we meet with a Collection of Scottish Prophecies (many of which are ascribed to Thomas the Rhymer) printed in the last years of the 16th cent., and being, although it must chiefly have been destined for the lower population, in as good English as many works printed to the South of the Tweed.

In the first years of the following century, the Scotch court was removed to England. And, although James, the first of England and the sixth of Scotland, still, at least to judge from the Fortunes of Nigel, "spak Braid Scotch," its doom was sealed as a language of Court and — Literature.

Abbreviations.

Al.: The buik of the most vailzand conquerour Alexander the Great. Edinburgh, 1831, 4:o.
Br.: The Bruce and (Wal.) Wallace. Published by Dr. J. JAMIESON. 2 vol. Edinburgh; 1820, 4:o.
Bel.: H. Boethii Cronyklis of Scotland, translatit by Bellenden. 1536; fol.
Ch.: The Canterbury Tales of Geoffrey Chaucer. A new text with illustrative notes by THOMAS WRIGHT. London and Glasgow. 8:o.
Cl.: Clariodus, a metrical Romance (ed. by DAV. IRVING). Edinb. 1830, 4:o.
Col.: Collections Relating to the History of Mary Queen of Scotland by JAMES ANDERSON Esq. 4 vol. Edinburgh, London, 1727—28; 4:o.
Db.: The Poems of William Dunbar. Edited by Mr. DAVID LAING. Edinburgh, 1834; 8:o.
Dig.: Ancient Mysteries from the Digby M. S. S. Edinb. 1835; 4:o.
Gaw.: Syr Gawayne; A Collection of Ancient Romance Poems by Scotish and English authors; ed. by Sir FRED. MADDEN. London 1839; 4:o. G. K.: Syr Gawayne and The Grene Knyzt; A. A.: The awntyrs of Arthure at the Terne Wathelyune; G. G.: The Knightly Tale of Golagros and Gawane.
Hm.: Hume (Alex.) Hymns and Sacred Songs. Edinb. 1832; 4:o.
Howl.: Holland: The buke of the Howlat; ed. by Mr. DAVID LAING. Edinb. 1823; 4:o.
Kn.: The works of John Knox; edited by Mr. DAVID LAING. Edinburgh 1846; 8:o.
Kng.: The Buke of the Order of Knyghthood. Translated from the French by Sir GILBERT HAY, Knight. Edinburgh, 1849; 4:o.
Le.: Leges quatuor burgorum. and A. R. W.: Assise Regis Willelmi, in: Acts of the Parliaments of Scotland, vol. 1.
Leg.: The Legend of St. Katherine from Alexandria. London, 1841; 4:o.
Ls.: The Poetical Works of Sir David Lyndsay of the Mount. Edited by George CHALMERS. London, 1806. 3 vol. 8:o.
Li.: Die Vier Evangelien in Alt-Nordhumbrischer Sprache. Herausgegeben von K. W. BOUTERWEK. Gütersloh, 1857; 8:o.

Li. St.: The Lindisfarne and (Rush.:) Rushworth Gospels. Ed. by Rev. Joseph STEVENSON. Durham 1854; 8:o.
Orm.: The Ormulum. Ed. by Rev. K. M. WHITE. Oxford, 1852. 2 vol. 8:o.
Pal.: Select Works of Gawin Douglas. Perth, 1787. 12:o.
(Ps.): (Anglo-Saxon and) Ps: Early English Psalter. Edit. by Rev. Joseph STEVENSON. London, 1843. 2 vol. 8:o.
Rit.: Rituale Ecclesiæ Dunelmensis. Ed. by Rev. Joseph Stevenson. Durham, 1840. 8:o.
Rob. and Mak.: Robine and Makyne by Robert Henryson. Edinburgh, 1824. 4:o.
S. S.: The sevin Seages by John Rolland. Edinburgh, 1837. 4:o.
Thorpe: þa Halgan Godspel on Englisc. Edited from the original M. S. S. by Benjamin THORPE, F. S. A. London, 1842; 8:o.
Vir.: Virgilii Æneis. Translated by Gawin Douglas. Edited by George DUNDAS and Andr. RUTHERFORD. Edinburgh 1839. 2 vol. 4:o. The quotations refer all to vol. 1.
W.: Wyntown's Orygynale Cronykil of Scotland. Edited by David M'PHERSON. London, 1795. 2 vol. 4:o and 8:o.
Y. M.: An extract from the York Mysteries printed in GARNETT'S Phil. Ess. p. 192. — A. S.: Anglo-Saxon. N. A.: North-Anglic. W. S.: West-Saxon. S. E.: Scoto-English

www.ingramcontent.com/pod-product-compliance
Lightning Source LLC
Chambersburg PA
CBHW032250080426
42735CB00008B/1072